A Celebration of Dogs

Roger Caras

Times
BOOKS

Also by Roger Caras:

Antarctica: Land of
   Frozen Time
Dangerous to Man
The Custer Wolf
Sarang
Monarch of Deadman Bay
Panther!

Source of the Thunder
The Private Lives of
   Animals
The Forest
Yankee
The Roger Caras
   Dog Book

Published by TIMES BOOKS, a division of
Quadrangle/The New York Times Book Co., Inc.
Three Park Avenue, New York, N.Y. 10016

Published simultaneously in Canada by
Fitzhenry & Whiteside, Ltd., Toronto

Library of Congress Cataloging in Publication Data

Caras, Roger A.
  A celebration of dogs.

  Includes index.
  1. Dogs. I. Title.
SF426.C336 1982 636.7   82–50083
ISBN 0–8129–1029–X

Book design by Jordan Brenner

Manufactured in the United States of America

He was vain, even arrogant, he was splendid, magnanimous, noble, he was utterly superb. He was Champion The Rectory's Yankee Patriot, a bloodhound. No one who knew him will ever forget him. His death at seven and a half was devastating. But the fact that he lived at all was a blessing and a miracle.

Foreword

I have heard it suggested that the author of a nonfiction book should be dispassionate, objective, unsentimental, and detached. In that way alone can he or she hope to lay truth, objectivity, and accuracy on the reader's plate. I have heard it suggested, with equal profundity, of course, that the author of any book had better be up to the neck (and heart) in the subject about which he or she is writing. In *that* way and that way alone can an author hope to hook, hold, and thereby serve the reader.

Rules like these sound good no matter what they say. I think that is very often true about profound statements. It doesn't matter a fig what they say, only how you say them. Oscar Wilde was on to something when he said that in matters of great importance it is style, not substance, that matters.

I am not dispassionate about dogs, nor do I intend to try

to be. Nothing I have to say in this book will be wholly objective, detached, or lacking in sentiment. I will certainly try to be accurate in all matters of which I have knowledge, and I will most certainly tell the truth as I have come to understand it. But I have quite literally been up to my neck and heart in dogs since before my memory registers, and in all sizes, shapes, and styles they have been part and parcel of my being.

Anyone who has been "into dogs" at all knows the truth of the premise suggested by the title of this book. They are a cause for celebration, they are a joy . . . but I am getting ahead of myself. If you want to share the world of dogs with me, if you want to think about them, perhaps worry about them a little, maybe even learn some new things about them, read on.

Roger Caras
East Hampton, New York
Spring 1982

Contents

1
The Dogs in Our Lives

If you don't own a dog, at least one, there is not necessarily anything wrong with you, but there may be something wrong with your life. If you've owned a dog, plan to own a dog, or even want to own a dog, it is almost as good as owning one—but nothing equals the joy of the experience itself. You surrender a lot, but what you gain is beyond measuring.

As I write this I am locked away in a kind of private dungeon, a soundproof room in the basement of our country house. It is a room that reflects my life as a naturalist. Bottles full of pickled snakes (including a fifteen-foot king cobra and an eleven-foot bushmaster), cases of butterflies, birds' eggs (snitched from nests decades before I was born by a Victorian nature enthusiast, not taken by me!), books, rocks, a marvelous letter written to me by Dr. Einstein in 1949 framed with an equally wonderful photograph of him with his messy bird's-nest hairdo—all kinds of scraps from a very full life that happily is still very much in progress. Although my wife, our kids, and I own about twenty pets, only three are allowed in this room, because some of the artifacts and specimens are poisonous and must not be investigated by nosy cats or pushy puppies. A splendid Mexican red-kneed tarantula lives in a twenty-gallon tank that has been converted to a desert terrarium. She is here full-time. The other two companions with special dispensation are a very large champion bloodhound named Yankee and a male golden retriever named Jeremy. The hound belongs to my son, who is away at medical school in Boston, and the retriever belongs to my daughter, who is away making her mark in the publishing industry. She has to travel, so Jeremy has remained behind where he was raised. That is true, of course, of Yankee as well.

The point to all this personal trivia? Jeremy and Yankee are my close personal friends. Really, actually that. They have not replaced human beings, not at all. They care about me a great deal and both understand and respond to me. These two big males don't fight, they don't grumble, they share this room and me. When I go to my study after breakfast, which will almost always be after they have had their morning run, they head down the stairs with me. They know. We have a lot of work to get done and we had better get cracking, the three of us. During the day I may want to read something out loud, particularly if it is a script for a broadcast. They listen patiently and at least try to look interested. They never criticize.

For most of the day they sleep, shifting, swapping positions, a rug for a chair and, depending on the season, a spot nearer to or farther from the heater or air conditioner, but this is where they spend their working hours, our working hours. Every hour or so (there is a pattern, but no fixed time element), one or the other will come over and sit beside me. If I keep typing or editing or find any other excuse for ignoring the opening bid, a paw or a chin lands on my knee and one eyebrow or the other goes up. Whichever dog is making the gesture is watched by the other. This is the one place where they compete, on the heart level. The chin or paw-on-knee gambit works, of course, and the offer is accepted and a moment or two taken out for interaction. The other dog stands that for as long as he can and then he too comes over and gets his share.

What is going on, of course, is an extremely ancient ritual. As will be examined in the pages ahead, it goes all the way back to the beginning of the dog itself, all the way back to the wolf. We can't say very much about the behavior of an extinct species further back on the canine family tree than the wolf, at least not with any degree of certainty. But what is happening here in this room is an invaluable aspect of wolf behavior that has lived on in our dogs, as basic to their species' interactive behavior as social grooming is to monkeys and apes and as herding is to hoofed animals. These two great dogs are acknowledging me as Alpha Dog, or, historically speaking, top wolf.

People who have enjoyed dogs rather more than they have thought about them might assume that the paw-on-the-knee gambit is just begging for a bit of scratching. No such thing. As wolves and as dogs in a pack they would sniff the leader of their pack (in a way I would rather they not sniff me), nibble his lip, lie down next to him and roll over, do all kinds of nice social things that seem to say, "I am yours, take me, extend to me whatever attention you can spare." A dog getting scratched is not like a friend with an itchy back who can't reach the spot with a ruler and im-

plores you for help; the dog is asking for a far greater
commitment than that. The dog is saying, "May I belong,
and will you tell me once again that I do?"

In this exchange there is no loss of dignity by either
species. I am certainly not surrendering anything, and neither is the dog. We are both reaffirming an ancient relationship by means of an equally ancient ritual. A very long time
ago man assumed responsibility for the genetic alteration of
a species of wolf because it pleased him to do so. Later on
he was to find he couldn't get along without that companion
carnivore, not and raise livestock and hold off competitors
for food and shelter. None of that would have been possible
if the wolf had not come from a social structure that called
for benevolent dominance. A "dog" from any other source
would probably not have served as well. There is nothing
accidental about where our dogs came from or what they
have come to be. It was part of the evolution of two inter-
locked species. We were one of them.

It is possible to overintellectualize, overanalyze any subject, but that is not what I intend to do here. I am aware of
the danger. Of course, many will argue, it is quite enough
to want to pat a dog that wants to be patted. But the prehistory of man and beast may very well be a part of it; everything that has gone before is part of everything we know,
do, are, or can ever hope to be. It is fun, too, if you care
about dogs, to care about our mutual history and know
something about it. Man arrived at his present high station
in life with the dog by his side. Socializing the wolf and
evolving the dog through selective breeding was one of the
first things man did as he began to emerge from the back
of the cave. Perhaps not because he had dogs but concur-
rent with his having them, man began to build the cultures
on which our lives today are founded. Before man had dog

—again, I am not necessarily implying cause so much as coincidence—he wasn't all that interesting a creature, not socially, not culturally. He was probably rather grim, probably humorless, and certainly a brutal survivalist. Little wonder. What he wasn't eating was eating him.

How much of a role the dog played in the evolution of human culture cannot now be determined. I doubt very much that it ever will be. If it is, it won't be by someone as sentimental, passionate, and involved as I. I would probably see a dog behind every temple pillar and under every bush brought to domestication by man on his way from gatherer to earth-scratcher to husbandryman to industrialist. We can, though, speculate for a moment or two. No harm in that.

Could man have survived the dangers of life twenty thousand years ago without the emerging dog to warn him of stealthy attackers in the night? Probably. Man wouldn't have been wiped out as a species, but a lot more men, women, and children might have died. To this day there is no reckoning how much property is saved and how much violence avoided simply because there is a dog around to make noise at the appropriate time.

Would man have survived as a sheep and goat herder without dogs? We have to slow down a bit here. It is quite possible that he wouldn't have. It is extremely unlikely that Stone Age or even Bronze Age man could have created traps that would have outwitted bears, cats, and wolves with any degree of regularity. It can be assumed that man that far back had a limited pharmacopoeia and had few effective poisons at his disposal. How then would he have protected his flocks in a world where the competition for protein was fierce? Sheep and goat herding would have been rough going without dogs. And later, when cattle were domesticated, droving dogs as well as guard dogs must have made larger herds a more viable idea. Since cattle have long been a form of exchange (they still are in many parts of Africa), the role of the dog in caring for livestock had more profound meaning than just feeding the folks at home. Cattle bought brides, brides had babies, and babies grew up to take care of their parents when they grew old. There is no way to quantify the role of the dog, but it is safe to surmise that everything in the cultural history of man that stemmed from the maintenance of livestock (including having wool to wear) was in no small part dependent on the dog. You don't have to spend too much time worrying about that just because you want to pat your dog, but there it is.

For millennia, human beings have lived in the Arctic and used it as an avenue of migration. It has been a very busy place, and sled dogs have been an essential element in man's ability to cope with the extraordinary rigors of that frozen world. In that one area dogs have been absolutely necessary. We may tend to think of the Eskimos themselves as unimportant to what we consider the mainstream of human development, but the migrations that brought man to the New World and allowed for mass movements across the top of the world cannot be dismissed. The Vikings, too, spread out and were among the first to begin peeling back the layers of the unknown that for so long had clouded our perception of our own planet. Sled dogs, northern spitz animals, made a great deal of it possible. In the south, in arid, semiarid, and temperate zones, they may or may not have been truly indispensable in the management of livestock. In the far north no such question exists: dogs were indispensable.

Clearly, I am not the one to ask for an objective evaluation of the role of dogs in the life of man. But I have been studying the subject all my life, just as I have been living it, and although I cannot give the mythical dispassionate view of this ancient love affair, I can remember some of its joys and share a little esoterica. Did you know, for example, that you will probably live longer, at least statistically, if you own dogs, one or more? Did you know that your blood pressure will be far easier to hold at a healthy level if you are a pet keeper than if you are not? Scientific studies bear this out. Pets are extremely good for your whole cardiovascular system, not to mention your psyche. You are less likely to commit suicide, less likely to take offense at what people do to you, if you have the leveling influence of a dog at some key points in the day to make the bad things go away. The dog does not judge you, and not being judged in the midst of our heavily judging and judged existence is like a life preserver in the middle of the sea. It virtually spells salvation for a great many people, especially young people being pulled at from all sides by peers, parents, teachers, and a blossoming libido.

What breed of dog most closely matches your personality and your needs? I will get into that and make a few suggestions. The biggest single problem facing any prospective dog owner is choice, because the range is so enormous within the infinitely variable species to which the domestic dog belongs, *Canis familiaris*. All domestic dogs belong to this single species, but if you need a Yorkshire terrier to round out your life a komondor just isn't going to do it for you; neither is a kerry blue terrier. Dogs and people are both so extraordinarily variable in their needs and in their ability to respond to needs that a good dog-person match is a gift of the heavens. It happens millions of times every year, but should be engineered to as large a degree as possible. A lot can be done to make sure a dog "works out."

When a dog is said not to work out it is invariably the dog that suffers. People don't move out of the house and leave it to the dog and his friends. The dog gets dumped, and in a dreadfully large number of cases that is a death sentence. It is terribly important that the prospective dog owner take the time to understand what is available and put it all together in not only an intelligent but a loving way. That is what all of this is all about—loving.

A word about dog people—and here we can give the dog full credit. Clearly, if there weren't dogs there couldn't be dog lovers, dog owners, or, collectively, dog people. At best they are a strange lot, dog people. An estimated 52 percent of the homes in America have dogs as regular members of the family, so there are a lot of them. They buy so much dog food (which has far better labeling standards than human food packages) that the dog-food industry has within the last few years become one of television's *major* advertisers. That puts the six-billion-dollar-a-year kibble-and-can industry on a par with automobiles, deodorants, and soda pop.

These buyers of dog food must spend a great deal of money on film and processing, because most of them are as quick to show you color snaps of their dogs as they are of their children. Our daughter insists we are even quicker to show the dog snaps and says that she was unlucky not to have been born a bloodhound. She engages in hyperbole, of course.

We will explore some of the intricacies of the bond that binds men, women, and children to a four-legged carnivore, but it is interesting, I think, that man selected two carnivores, two hunting animals, the dog and the cat, to bond to most strongly. Horse people, it is true, are hardly less irrational about their horses than dog and cat people are about their pets, but for obvious reasons concerning economics, exercise demands, and space, horses are rather fewer in number around the home. Why no monkeys? Why didn't early man pick animals more like himself, animals that are demonstrably more intelligent than either the dog or the cat (which, apparently, are about equal in intelligence)? The answer will emerge, I hope, later on.

The way man deals with his dogs is not uniformly pleasant. But that too will be dealt with. It makes one want to celebrate dogs all the more.

Look on this book as a celebration, as an example of joy. We derive immeasurable good, uncounted pleasures, enormous security, and many critical lessons about life by owning dogs. It is an ancient, venerable, honorable, and altogether delightful practice. It has its problems, but so do marriage and childrearing. It has its costs, but so does virtually everything we do, and certainly everything that brings us even occasionally to the edge of ecstasy. I don't know what life would have been like for the last fifteen thousand years or more without dogs except that it would have been different. In all likelihood, we would be emotionally different, our life expectancy would be different, and our economic structures would be different.

Dogs have always subsisted on handouts. We give them the love we can spare, the time we can spare, the room we can spare. Even the best of the balanced dog foods, although meticulously compounded, consist of what we can spare from the slaughterhouse and what we can grow on the land we can spare. In return, dogs have given us their absolute all. We are the center of their universe, we are the focus of their love and faith and trust. They serve us in return for scraps. It is without a doubt the best deal man has ever made.

2

How It May Have Started

Before there was a man-dog relationship there obviously had to be both men and women, and dogs. Men and women came first, at least before the dog we keep today as a companion animal. The far older dogs of Asia and Africa, as I will explain, probably played no role at all in the coming of Spot or Fido.

The epoch we call the Eocene began approximately fifty million years ago and lasted for perhaps twenty million years. It was during that time that a beast known as *Miacis* emerged. It was a combination of weasel, cat, bear, and dog; in short, it was an extremely primitive carnivorous type. It had a future, however. It had promise because it contained a lot of good mammalian ideas.

Starting thirty-five million years ago, for a period lasting almost fifteen million years, there was the epoch called the Oligocene. It was during that period that *Miacis* gave way to several even better ideas. There was *Daphnaenus,* an animal much heavier than its ancestor *Miacis* had been. From *Daphnaenus* would one day come all of the bears. There was a lighter-boned descendant of *Miacis* known as *Cynodictis,* and from it would come the dog family. It was at that point, when *Daphnaenus* and *Cynodictis* coexisted, that the dogs and bears split for all time. *Cynodesmus* was next in line after *Cynodictis.* It was more doglike yet. The weasels and cats that had also arisen from *Miacis* were headed off on their own, like the bears. The hyenas, more catlike than doglike anatomically, were also split off and were edging away from the line of canine descent. The meat-eaters were becoming more and more differentiated, more specialized. The dinosaurs were gone, the mammals had inherited the earth. With their superior brains they were exploring every niche and trying on all shapes and sizes.

The Miocene epoch dawned about twenty million years ago and was destined to last for close to thirteen million years. Man was still about seventeen million years in the future, but *Cynodesmus* had already evolved to *Tomarctus,* and from that animal the wolves, foxes, wild dogs, and jackals would eventually arise. In at least one of them our pet dog of today was hidden. All kinds of canines came and went, new ideas replaced old ones, and the line continued its refinement. Parallel tracks were laid down, but it was within the wolf that lay the dog man would one day extract, polish, and eventually cherish. That is where the dog's story starts, roughly fifty million years after the mists of eternity produced *Miacis* and a couple of million years after the man-idea pushed apes upright, moved their spinal column forward under their skull, straightened out their bowed knees, and made their thumbs grow. We know rather less about the details than we would like, but we have the results all around us, and that, surely, is far more important.

To pinpoint the actual beginning of the man-dog relationship requires a good bit of conjecture, as do most things that happened between one hundred and two hundred centuries ago. In most parts of the world the dog was probably the first domestic animal man extracted from the living forms around him. There seems to be little argument on that point. Most likely it happened somewhere in the Middle East or southwestern Asia. The date suggested for the event is often fourteen thousand years B.P. (before the present). That may be a modest estimate, since man had purebred dogs seven thousand years ago in America, and the remaining seven thousand years seems a fairly short time for that level of technical accomplishment to be arrived at in the Stone Age and that much traveling to have been done. In fact, how people who couldn't write and probably had more fleas than their dogs mastered selective breeding is thoroughly confounding.

The first issue, however, is how and why it happened. Man the carnivore—more properly the omnivore, because he was surely hunting, gathering, and eating everything in sight, including his neighbor in some instances—appears to have suddenly reached out and taken a fellow carnivore and therefore competitor into the cave and made him a partner. All this with no history or tradition of domestication. It almost seems as if there had to have been some kind of revelation.

There have been any number of romanticized views of how it came to pass. One day Mrs. Flintstone supposedly said something to the effect that the kids would love a puppy and Fred should bring one home from work. Unlikely.

Slightly more plausible, but still probably less than likely, is the idea that some small species of wolf not unlike one still to be found from India to Israel and probably once even more widely distributed than that (*Canis lupus pallipes*) began hanging around human dwellings to get the offal tossed aside by the hunting families and clans. Eventually, the theory goes, it became a habit for man and wolf to stay near each other, and it stuck and went on from there. Possible, but again I think unlikely.

What does seem likely is that man had a hard time making ends meet and brought home everything he could chew and swallow. There was a constant plaint back at the nest: more food, more food! A raid on a wolf den when the adults were away or had been neutralized with a shower of rocks would have periodically yielded a batch of tender puppies. Dogs are still eaten in Asia, so I have no problem with this speculation so far. Even cavemen would have discovered that meat goes high if it is dead and cannot be kept cold. Meat on the hoof stays fresh. It is my guess that pre-dog man began keeping puppies from kidnapped wolf litters around for food as needed. It is not difficult to imagine that sooner or later some kid would ask some father to spare a puppy. It was probably done as a temporary measure, but a habit came into being with which we are still enchanted. That little scene in the cave, however, is still a long way from purebred dogs genetically engineered to fulfill a job like sheepherding or game tracking or guard duty. There was still a way to go. A wolf puppy cannot grow up to be a dog no matter how much you love it.

And what does the record show? For a long time it was assumed that there were two ancestors to the dog, the wolf and the jackal. That has pretty much gone by the way, although wolves, jackals, and domestic dogs can all interbreed. There is a lot of liberal democracy in the canine genetic package. But the wolf generally gets full credit today for giving us our dogs. Large wolves come from the northern latitudes and smaller wolves from southern ones, so the southern wolf, as suggested a moment ago, again generally gets most of the credit. I personally believe that the larger northern wolf figures in the ancestry of northern spitz-like dogs, but for the mainstream of domestic dog development I would accept that little southerly wolf, because there isn't really very much more we have to go with.

Where? Certainly not in any one place. An idea that has been good enough to last for one to two hundred centuries was almost certainly good enough to have more than one inventor. There were, in all likelihood, many places where the socialization of wolf began, and many places where the idea caught on.

When scientists dig up ancient human sites, how do they know if they are finding wolf remains or dog remains? That certainly is a significant point if one wants to claim that a particular race of people had dogs. It isn't as difficult as it may seem. Strange things happen to canines when they are domesticated. Sad to relate, but unavoidably true, is the fact that their brains shrink. A dog's brain is 20 to 30 percent smaller than that of a wolf the same size. Teeth become more crowded as muzzles shorten. Wolves and dogs, even in the earliest stages of domestication, can almost always be distinguished from each other. Paleontologists have little trouble making a determination.

Unexpectedly—bewilderingly, in fact—the single earliest domestic dog so far known was found in the New World, not the Old. In Birch Creek Valley in Idaho there is an archaeological site known as Jaguar Cave, and there, roughly 10,500 years ago, there were men with small dogs that had short, broad muzzles. The premolars of those dogs were crowded, proving to virtually everyone's satisfaction that this was indeed a dog and not a wolf. At least as interesting is the fact that these dogs show every sign of having been descended from the Old World wolves, not any wolf species found in North America. They were a long way from home. These were dogs that came to this hemisphere from Asia, although it was probably much farther west, where Europe meets Asia, that dogs first began to emerge, those small-brained wolves whose teeth were being crowded into an ever shortening muzzle. There are no details about that incredible trek. It is a long way from Jericho to Idaho. What happened to the dog along the way, and what happened to man?

In Europe itself there are clear records of dogs in Germany, in a place called Senckenberg Bog in Frankfurt am Main. They date from about 9,500 years ago. In the British Isles there were dogs in a place called Starr Carr. The dogs in England seem to have been more advanced than their German counterparts, although the German and English finds are from about the same time. Since it is highly likely that early dog owners allowed the influx of wolf blood from time to time (Eskimos have done that with their sled dogs to the present day), the relative primitiveness of a specimen or two from a hundred centuries ago may not tell us very much about when dogs started or where. We are dealing, it must be remembered, with a skimpy record and a lot of guesswork.

In Anatolia, Turkey's hind foot in Asia, there were dogs at least nine thousand years ago, particularly at a place called Cayonu. It is possible, just possible, that in some isolated areas sheep or goats or perhaps even both were domesticated a little earlier than dogs. Generally, though, dogs were the first animals domesticated, or rather wolves were socialized and dogs later evolved from them.

What those early dogs looked like is hard to say. The domestic canine is an amazingly flexible genetic package, and all manner of variations have come and gone. Those at the beginning are particularly difficult to identify. In the newer Stone Age sites in Switzerland there appears a dog variously known as the turbary dog or turbary spitz. It was spitz-like; it was quite small, certainly smaller than the wolf from which it was descended; and it had a spacious brain case, which probably meant it was a smart little animal not far removed from its genetic origins. Its remains are found in Neolithic sites scattered all over Switzerland and in other parts of Europe as well. There were at least two other larger dogs in Switzerland at the same time, indicating that even Stone Age man had his choice of breeds. There were a variety of dogs in Russia at the same time, perhaps already doing different kinds of jobs for their owners.

Thus, ten thousand years ago men in several states of technological development had dogs not of one kind but of several. Some scientists believe they can ascribe work types to these dogs. Some seem to have been bred for hunting and others for herding. Some of the individual conclusions drawn may be less than totally sound, but the story as a whole seems clear. A hundred centuries ago, men of very little technological sophistication and probably next to no knowledge of biology were selectively breeding dogs. How is a mystery; why seems obvious. If we knew more about the history of dogs, it seems clear, we would know more about the history of man.

It is said that mankind now doubles his technological skill every five years in a kind of intellectual inflation. At the time I am speaking of, one hundred centuries ago, it supposedly took man thousands of years to achieve the equivalent doubling. Allowing that such figures are probably fairly loose, it would still mean that if ten thousand years ago man was selectively breeding for breed types he must have had dogs around for a very long time before that. When his canid companions actually crossed over and became dogs can never be established with precision, so a good part of that earlier time may have been a matter of keeping cleverly socialized wolves. My conclusion is that man and canine have been companions for a period that could cover two hundred and fifty centuries, twenty-five thousand years. Very few human cultural complexes would have preceded that. Dog-keeping or at least wolf-about-to-be-dog-keeping may be the fourth oldest of all our cultural activities. Hunting and gathering, lumped together as a single activity, and perhaps storytelling came earlier. Fire almost certainly came next. Man had to eat before he could keep pets. As suggested earlier, it was probably his eating habits that triggered the first pet-owning that man ever attempted.

In China today dogs can be classified into fairly well-defined groups. The distinctions that can be observed there are truly ancient. There were at least four main lines.

There is a generalized pariah dog in China. It is a relatively primitive, unrefined dog, not at all unlike dogs still found around African villages and over much of India. Some tend toward the shepherd type of head with a fair brain capacity, some toward the greyhound narrow head, and some are spitz-like and suggest the input of what we now call the chow chow. Actually, the name "chow chow" is not used in China. It is generally believed that that name

arose among European traders as a pidgin phrase meaning
"bric-a-brac." When European trade ships arrived in China
to load up with pottery, porcelain, carved wooden screens,
silks, and brocades, they took dogs along to sell in receptive
western marketplaces. The dogs, like the rest of the cargo,
were called chow chow. The term actually referred to any
Chinese dog. So the story goes, at least.

The pariah dog has been used for food throughout much
or all of its history. Eating dog is a very ancient Chinese
custom and has both practical and religious origins. Puppies are typically fattened on a rice gruel and slaughtered
at nine to ten months of age.

In Kirin Province, near the Korean border, somewhat
larger dogs than those found in the south are still kept for
food, and although they are pariah dogs too, they are more
refined and have longer coats to suit the colder climate. The
northern pariah dogs have a shepherd-like head, those farther south are either terrier-like or spitz-like. These are very
generalized descriptions, of course. In Korea itself, a kind
of yellow-and-white pariah dog (it is occasionally found with
black fur) is also raised for food. This practice and these
dogs conceivably go back to the origin of dog-keeping itself.
In fact, I find it very hard to believe that Stone Age man had
any luxuries at all, and inedible animals would have been
luxuries, particularly if they themselves required feeding.

In Yunnan Province, in Kwangtung and Kwangsi, are
found distinct dogs of the pariah type maintained for food
and in some cases for hunting. There is no telling when any
of the practices now connected with them began. Most experts concede that the pariah type or edible dog is China's
oldest.

The chow chow or spitz-like dogs make up China's second basic canine group. Why the chow chow is the only dog

in the world with a black tongue is not clear, but it is certainly clear that the dog is no more closely related to the bear than any other breed, despite claims to the contrary. In various parts of China the chow chow is called the *lanfkou* (wolf dog), the *hsiungkou* (bear dog), the *hei she-t'ou'* (black-tongued dog), and the *kwang-tung-kou* (dog of Kwangtung).

Other Chinese dogs are best described as shepherds. The shepherd type does not necessarily mean something that looks like the German shepherd or "police dog" of today; it more often refers to a mastiff-like animal with a more massive head. In Manchuria, Mongolia, Sinkiang, Tibet, and other Asian pastoral regions, large working dogs emerged. How and when they migrated westward cannot be said, but it was surely one of the many stocks from which many of today's European breeds emerged. In both Manchuria and Mongolia, brides were expected to raise long-haired dogs and got breeding stock as part of their dowries. They raised them as a cash crop. In the not too recent past, dog coats were shipped to markets in both Europe and the United States. Raising dogs for pelts was an ancient practice and undoubtedly still goes on. We think of dogs as companions or at least helpers. That has not been universally true. In Asia, intense affection and the most appalling cruelty have dwelt comfortably side by side.

A clear line of descent for Chinese dogs was the true mastiff, probably the product of both Tibet and Mongolia. They were giants, and records of them can be traced back over three thousand years. There were clearly defined breeds even then, and they were objects of a profitable trade.

The greyhound was found in ancient China as it was throughout the Middle East, in Rome, and everywhere civilization emerged. The value of a tough coursing hound is obvious, and whether the greyhound, one of the very oldest of all breeds, was used primarily for sport or food-getting probably depended on the time and the place. But Chinese art depicts the breed as being not very different from what it is now.

At least a thousand years before the beginning of the Christian era there were toy dogs in China, and they could have had only one possible use. They were companions and were probably treated as small works of art by the wealthy (even as now). There are stories of later Chinese emperors employing human wet nurses for their dogs, and it is possible that the infants of peasant girls were killed to save milk for the dogs. How obscene the methods employed to maintain favored toy dogs three thousand years ago in Asia is anyone's guess. In China the toys were often referred to as sleeve dogs, because they were carried in the cavernous sleeves of wealthy collectors and fanciers. But whether the practice of stunting dogs by selective breeding began in Asia is not known. By the time Pompeii was obliterated, the Italian greyhound, surely a companion toy, was already in existence.

Many of today's familiar breeds began in China as companions of the rich and noble, among them pekingese, pug, Tibetan terrier, and Lhasa apso. Some, like the Japanese chin, were refined in Japan after being shipped there from China, but early in the history of man and dog the peoples of the Far East were breeding small jewels whose only purpose could have been to please a highly developed aesthetic sense. How the small wolf of India and the Middle East got to the Far East no one knows. By the thirteenth century when Marco Polo got there, however, changes had been made, for he wrote of dogs four feet tall at the shoulder. Between a four-foot-tall mastiff and a diminutive sleeve dog there had to have been a lot of breeding, a lot of differences in taste, style, and need, and a great deal of elapsed time.

Africa poses an interesting problem. Dogs are datable all over that vast area back to some of the earliest known human settlements. But there are no wolves on that continent and probably never have been. There are jackals of several species, but they have been pretty well eliminated as being ancestral to these dogs. Early dogs in ancient Africa meant trade, not jackal genes. Dogs were obviously objects of trade at a very early stage in peripatetic man's sea and overland journeys. That suggests the regard in which they were held. You took along only what you needed, loved, or could sell when you traversed the "dark continent" before it was illuminated.

The pariah dog of Africa was widespread at the same time the pariah dog of China was being boiled up with dried mushrooms and ginger, at the same time Tibetan mastiffs were guarding narrow passes and Norwegian elkhounds were setting forth with Viking raiders and explorers. In the Sahara there were pariah dogs, and I have seen rock drawings of them in the heart of the Sinai Peninsula, in a high mountain pass called Waki Mukateb. No one knows who made the drawings or when, but they did have dogs as well as horses and camels.

There were berber dogs in Libya, Algeria, and Morocco, refinements of the pariah type. And there *may* have been an ancestral type known as the armenti dog on the left bank of the Nile. That is a problem dog, because there are stories that the armenti has been there only since Napoleon's troops dropped some off at the turn of the nineteenth century. Other accounts have a Russian traveler packing guard dogs with him, some of which became the armenti of Egypt. It is more likely, however, that the breed goes back much further than the beginning of the nineteenth century and was derived from the pariahs that had been spread all across the north of Africa.

Dogs similar to the armenti were found in Ethiopia and farther south in East Africa. In the Congo there were bright little pariah dogs that many people say gave rise to the basenji we know today. Other experts place the basenji first in Egypt and only later in the Congo.

All the way south, to the southern tip of Africa, in fact, there were pariah dogs in ancient times. Bantu peoples used them as hunting companions, and in Southwest Africa there were what we today call hottentot dogs. Interestingly enough, these pariah-dog derivatives seem to have had greyhound blood mixed in. The dogs found in the Kalahari and Namib deserts today have probably not been there long. The Bushmen almost certainly got them from white men within the last two or three centuries.

By the time the pharaohs ruled Egypt, pariah dogs were common and probably prowled around every village seeking offal. Many of them were mummified, so they were certainly kept as pets by at least some segments of the population. On a recent trip to Central Soviet Asia, specifically Turkmenistan, I saw large numbers of pariah dogs. At night their yapping and squabbling made sleep difficult. This was particularly true in Ashkabad, twenty-five kilometers from the Iranian border, so I assume the same populations prevail to the south and beyond. How many of these animals there are in North Africa and the Middle East is impossible to know.

Even today, North African peoples generally hold pariah dogs in enormous contempt. The world of Islam is very hard on dogs unless they are of the greyhound type, breeds like the swift and graceful saluki and the afghan hound.

Pariah dogs were considered dirty through most of the recorded history of the region, and it can be assumed that the prejudice goes back further than those records. Although I have never heard anyone use it, there is supposedly a Moslem saying that "a saluki can share the tent of a king," presumably revealing the esteem with which greyhound-like dogs have always been held by desert peoples. I have seen how badly pariah dogs are treated in many parts of Africa and Asia as well as in the Middle East, enough to know that if one were to believe in reincarnation a pariah dog would be a disastrous choice for one's next trip through.

Every now and then the term "tesem hound" pops up in readings in archaeology. This was a greyhound-like dog from Egypt, perhaps the earliest dog recorded there. It first appears on a pottery bowl, in fact, four of them do, all walking demurely on leashes. The bowl is about six thousand years old. If the breed was distinct, leashed, represented on pottery, and obviously well established six thousand years ago, how long before that did greyhound-like dogs reach Egypt? No answer, but not long after that, tesem-like dogs were found in South and Southwest Africa. The coursing hound has been considered not only a good idea but a regal one since the birth of dogdom.

Before the great dynasties emerged in Egypt, the mastiff had reached the region. During the early dynasties the guard and shepherding dogs familiar in Mongolia and Tibet were on pottery. It isn't known how much breeding was done and how many dogs were brought in as trade items. Characteristically, early traders in highly desirable breeds of dogs would have made only one sex available. If you want a type of dog badly enough, however, you can reconstruct it with specimens of only one sex by breeding them with the nearest thing you can find to their type until you have pretty much duplicated the original. Since a generation can be a year or less, that need not be as prolonged a task as one might imagine.

As for the mastiff, it apparently did not do well in the Nile Valley, for it died off there while types that had been there long before thrived and still thrive to this day.

A native African breed well known now in the United States and Europe is the Rhodesian ridgeback, the dog with a cowlick of hair growing the wrong way along its spine. It is not an ancient breed at all, but was introduced and developed in the southern third of Africa by European settlers. Imported mastiffs, hounds, and possibly bird dogs figured in their early history. Hottentot dogs from the region contributed the cowlicks. The origin of that unique characteristic is unknown.

The pariah dogs of Africa often bear a strong resemblance to the coyote-sized dingo of Australia, which undoubtedly was a pariah dog carried to that continent and to New Zealand by early ocean travelers. The dingo died out in New Zealand but persisted in Australia, where it is often mistakenly thought of as a wild dog. It is not; it is a feral dog, one once domesticated. The dingo has had numerous parallels, including the pariah dogs of Africa. There are differences between the skulls of the true pariah dog and the dingo, but that is a result of life-style. The dingo hunts its prey as its ancestors the wolves did. Pariah dogs scavenge and therefore have lighter skulls. They can afford to, since they don't have to outwit prey and kill it.

Nothing illustrates the incredible spread of the domestic dog more clearly than the fact that dogs were waiting for European explorers when they reached the isolated islands of the Pacific. Captain Cook found them waiting for him on

Tahiti. They were in the Sandwich Islands (now Hawaii) before Europeans got there, and the speculation is that they came from India. Stone Age dogs from Europe were in New Guinea at almost the same time, which is also confounding. These are two fascinating points. Early man was capable of such journeys *and* he always seemed to take his dog along.

The shy, short-coated tengger dog is a little more difficult than the rest to explain. It existed in the eastern mountains of Java and may have been a true wild animal, not a descendant of the wolf and not a part of the mystifying flow of domestic dogs around the world. Some investigators say it was something else, a link between the dingo in Australia and the pariah dogs of Asia. It may have been part of the mainstream, or it may have been an aside to the history of the domestic dog. It simply is not known.

And so the story goes. There are sites in Austria and Hungary seven to ten thousand years old with distinctly different kinds of canine fossils. In Germany of that time a culture known as the Linear Pottery Culture had dogs ranging in size from the fox terrier to today's German shepherd. Dogs, there can be little doubt, for different uses, but all still apparently descended from that small Indian to Middle Eastern wolf; dogs on their way toward the enormous diversity known today. In the United States today there are 137 breeds and varieties recognized by the American Kennel Club in New York City and a dozen or so others recognized by the United Kennel Club in Kalamazoo, Michigan. There are hundreds of other breeds recognized around the world, many, perhaps most, of which may never be recognized here because as individual breeds they will not inspire the following that would warrant recognition.

So, from those early beginnings to today the dog has been not only our most consistent domestic animal but our most elastic one. In what other species taken into our lives can you find such variability: chihuahua, St. Bernard, Yorkshire terrier, Irish wolfhound, kerry blue terrier, samoyed, borzoi, toy poodle? Every one of them belongs to the same species, and all are in a direct line of descent from those Neolithic cave companions that were already well on their way to incredible diversity. A point to keep in mind, a sad one really, is that most of the breeds man has devised are extinct. Extant now are only a remnants of the historical breeds, because many of them were no more than points along the way, stages in an experiment, and although some surely lasted for centuries they are gone. What happened, for example, to the old English black-and-tan terrier that was probably ancestor to so many of today's terrier breeds?

Almost a thousand years ago there was a movement of dogs from the Iberian Peninsula, Spain and Portugal, northward. These "dogs of Spain" became known as spaniels, and they were split into two groups: basically the land dogs or setters, and some smaller version used on land and in the water—the spaniels. Where are most of them in their intermediate forms? As extinct as the dodo, and that analogy is not a bad one. Domestic animals are often as seriously endangered as wildlife. Man is always letting even its own creations slip away, and indeed that has been the case since the earliest dog breeders of the Stone Age matched dog to bitch, although heaven alone knows what they had in mind when they did it.

For reasons not yet understood, the size of dogs tended to increase during the Bronze Age. There were two other related developments as well. There appear to be more examples of dogs with skulls cut, split, or crushed, suggesting that man was eating dogs and that brains were a preferred food. Entirely likely. Is that why they liked bigger dogs? The other development is that dogs were now found buried with their masters. In some areas of Central Europe nearly half the dog bones available for study came from human burial sites. There is a mix that needs explaining. It is possible that some men thought so highly of their dogs that they were buried with them, and yet there is little doubt that these same men or their relatives ate dogs. It is unlikely that there was a cultural split, the dog eaters vs. the dog lovers. What is far more likely is that there were different kinds of dogs, the kinds you ate and the kinds you took to your grave with you. Another possibility: men may have loved dogs enough to be buried with them, but ate them in bad times. So far we have not been able to correlate famine and dog remains in kitchen middens. Of course, there is always the possibility that dogs were buried to feed the soul of the deceased on its journey to whatever hereafter was then in vogue. There is not yet a way of authentically characterizing a dog-human burial. Favorite dog? Symbolic guard and companion? Some combination of the above? Human slaves were certainly buried with their masters in Egypt. It does not take very much imagination to extend that to dogs, but it takes a lot of imagination as well as nerve to suggest that you know why it was done so long ago.

Dog-eating in Europe appears to have peaked during the Bronze Age. By the time the Iron Age was well advanced there was deliberate breeding of dwarf dogs, toys as they would be called today. They wouldn't have been meaty enough to waste time on, and they were too small for herding and certainly no good for hunting. They had to be companions. There were lap dogs in the Iron Age, no doubt about it.

During the period of the Roman Empire, up until its dissolution after the death of Christ, breeding dogs was

very serious business. There were dachshunds, greyhounds, salukis (and up in Siberia there were surely
samoyeds by then). All over the world, in fact, dogs were
being bred to specific styles. The mastiff-like dogs of Tibet
were well established. Sled dogs were in use, and the
Norwegian elkhound, another northern spitz-like animal,
was the companion of the Vikings on land and at sea and
in the afterworld. The Romans must have had a wide variety
of dogs. They had some the size of fox terriers, and some
clearly were dachshunds. They had racing dogs that were
probably nearly identical with the modern greyhound, and
of course the Egyptians had long since made Anubis a god.
That dog, as the pharaoh dog, a smooth-coated, sharp-
snouted hound, still survives. The dog now seen in American dog shows known as the ibizan hound was a close ally,
and the afghan hound had by then made it to Afghanistan,
where it was coursing leopard and gazelle. The saluki probably dates back to Sumeria nine thousand years ago and was
to be cherished throughout the Arab world. In the single
settlement of Tac in Pannonia (a Roman province in Central Europe) there were at least five or six dog breeds.

Of course, Europe and the Middle East were not areas of
quiet, stable societies. Peoples swept back and forth in vast
swarms and migrations. They took their dogs along either
because they ate them or because they wanted to be buried
with them, or to guard their camps against unfriendly locals,
and certainly to help herd the sheep and drive the cattle that
were taken along on any mass movement. Living off the
land was not possible when thousands of people were involved. And the movement of huge herds and flocks required dogs.

Dogs were lost, stolen, or just drifted away from cam-
paigns that failed or camps that fell to raiders. New mixtures

were inevitable, and the feral dog took up the niche left
vacant as the wolf population diminished. One thing man
the herder has always done is drive off the wolves that were
ancestral to his dogs, using his dogs, very often, for the task.

When the Romans crossed the Alps, they took mastiff-like
camp guards with them. The St. Bernard, the Bernese
mountain dog, and the rottweiler undoubtedly are some of
the many descendants of those dogs. The great dane (a
German breed, not a Danish one) also came down from
those mastiffs. To show how widespread dogs were in ancient times, the mastiffs the Romans had with them were
almost surely descended from imports from Asia, perhaps
as far away as Mongolia or Tibet. Yet when the Romans got
to the British Isles, they found the residents there equipped
with other mastiff-like dogs ready to fight alongside their
masters. The dogs went with the invaders, certainly, but in
many cases got there ahead of them. How and when isn't
known.

And so it went. Probably starting somewhere near the
Caspian Sea and a score of other places as well, probably
occurring anywhere from twelve to twenty-five thousand
years ago, small wolves were taken, socialized, acclimated,
then bred selectively. What inspired the early experiments
cannot be imagined, given the level of scientific sophistication then available. Genetic traits, gene pools, in- and out-
breeding could hardly have been understood by the people
who were in fact using them. What helped, of course, were
the facts that the dog matures quickly (less than a year) and,
if the bitch's comfort is not held in high regard, nor her
longevity, two litters of pups can be obtained a year. The
fact that the results of those early experiments reached Australia, Hawaii, Tibet, and the middle of North America as
early as they did speaks for remarkable movements. In fact,

one key to the movements of early man might be the distri-
bution of dogs, if dog types could ever be unraveled and
dated with relatively small margins of error. Since so many
breeds and types are known to us only as bone fragments,
we may be a long way from making all this clear enough to
be the kind of key we need. But the cyno-key, if it ever
emerges, could turn man's prehistory into history.

There *was* a great shuffling back and forth, there *was* a lot
of specialized breeding that could only have started as trial
and error (probably nothing but accident even before that),
but the wolf and probably the wolf alone was socialized, its
brain made smaller, its muzzle made shorter, its teeth
crowded in, and we got the dog. It is a gift from ancient
times that brings with it far more questions than answers.
So be it. We do not know the full story, we never can, but
we do have it today, the domestic dog, *Canis familiaris,* a
genetic miracle that has spread to every corner of earth
bringing joy wherever it has gone.

3
The Bonding

It would be absurd to think that man's interest in dogs remained strictly culinary or in any other way utilitarian for any appreciable length of time. Archaeological sites yield toy breeds and companions very early in the dog's career, and all of the rest of the history of man and dog over much of the world reveals a phenomenon known as bonding. Men bond with men, with women, women bond with men, with women; that is obviously known. What only animal lovers themselves may really appreciate is that human beings bond with nonhuman beings. It must be acknowledged here that what I am about to say for dogs is as true for cat lovers, horse lovers, anyone who finds a nonhuman companion fulfilling. But dogs are pack animals (just as horses are herd animals) and have a compelling instinct to fit into a structured situation. That and their size make them easy for us to relate to.

Amazingly enough, this fact was barely examined until recent times. The Old Testament did suggest, "A just man regardeth his beast," and Jews and Christians ever since have been trying desperately to show that this proves a humane ethic comes down to us from the Bible while all the while wallowing in a sea of animal agony caused by or at least allowed by man. In fact, until recently, dogs were taken for granted. They were always here; no human being alive could ever remember anyone who could remember a time when they weren't here, so in western cultures, at least, next to no thought was given the matter. Either you liked dogs or you didn't. Either you had dogs or you didn't. There was nothing more to it than that unless you bet on them in fights or races, neither event inspiring sentimentality. But stop and think about that for a moment.

As suggested earlier, a vast array of cultural complexes arose and most died since the first dogs were selectively bred during Mesolithic times. Human sacrifice was a perfectly valid form of propitiating the gods, or at least the natural forces that seemed to have the power to make things good or bad in a most whimsical fashion. It arose after dog-breeding had been established, because there wasn't any religion as we understand it before that, but that has gone by the way. Slavery came and went, although that was a valid economic device as long as you were the slaver and not the slavee. Cannibalism has vanished from a protein-starved world, but dog-keeping has hung on. Only one major religion, Islam, has not been accommodating to dogs. Virtually no forms of government have found dogs a poor idea except in isolated instances and then usually for a short period of time. Iceland once did not permit pet dogs; you had to have sheep and needed dogs as helpers in the pasture. In short, dogs have been acknowledged tacitly or by decree as a good idea almost as far back as any shovel can reveal.

What is behind it? Bonding. Call it love, call it whatever you wish, but don't suggest misanthropy. Psychiatrists have so long since proved that dog lovers are not people haters that whoever first made the silly suggestion must be bruised from turning in his or her grave. And what is the nature of the bond?

First, dogs are nonjudgmental. It doesn't matter where you are in your own personal development, nor has it mattered where you have been culturally; dogs simply don't pass judgment on you the way all of the rest of life and all of your other companions seem to. Miss a spear throw, the gazelle get away, going home empty-handed? Your dog will feel the pinch in his tummy as much as anyone else in the cave, but the dog won't whisper behind your back and blame you. Reputation and respect were probably as important in a cave as they are in a condominium. When men and women fail at something they generally have a reserve of paranoia to draw upon. We are all capable of being paranoid, and it never feels good. Dogs do not summon up that reserve. Flunk a French exam, hell coming at you from all quarters? Your dog couldn't care less. Get fired, cheat at cards or on a higher plane? Your dog will give you exactly the same greeting. The nonjudgmental quality of animal companions, the dog always having been the most popular of that group, is a major source of strength for the glue that binds us to so unlikely a friend. Unlikely? Four-legged, dependent, capable of transmitting one of history's most dread diseases, rabies, nonverbal, of a much lower intelligence, yet adored. Unlikely, but adored to the point of near ecstasy by some people and by some cultures.

The fact is that people do better when bonded. People

who live alone do not usually live as long as people who have a satisfactory relationship with someone or something else. Single people die earlier than married people, on the national average. Single people who live alone get sick more often than solidly bonded people and suffer more severe cases of the diseases they get. All of this has been known for some time. What no one seemed to notice before a couple of years ago was that people bonding to dogs (and other pets) experience pretty much the same effects. There may be differences in degree, but dogs do very well by us.

In 1980, four authors at the University of Pennsylvania published a paper called "Pet Ownership and Survival After Coronary Heart Disease." The authors, Dr. Erika Friedmann, Aaron Katcher, James Lynch, and Sue Ann Thomas, had come up with some startling facts about heart-attack victims.

The findings showed that if you had heart trouble you would probably have a much better chance of surviving for a longer period of time if you were bonded to a companion animal than if you weren't. Fifty-three people, each of whom had had a single heart attack, were placed in one group. Each of them either had a pet or was given one. Of those fifty-three people, three died within the first year of the study from a second heart attack. In the control group, thirty-nine people without pets were watched. In that same one-year period, eleven died of a second heart attack. Three out of fifty-three as compared with eleven out of thirty-nine: those are not mortality figures easily ignored. It could have been argued that the people with pets survived because they walked their dogs, and walking is very good for most heart-attack victims. To offset that possibility a number of the fifty-three were given pets that made no physical demands, like cage birds and guinea pigs. What was shown was that people are much healthier and much happier when involved with animals than when they are living alone.

What I find amazing is that anyone finds this amazing. As a child of ten I am certain that if I had been told of another kid down the street who was in a wheelchair and who was isolated and lonely I would have automatically said, "Get him a puppy." Of course, I was always up to my ears in puppies, kittens, turtles, snakes, and about everything else that could be crammed into a house and yard.

Studies in Maryland in the past few years revealed that people with explosively high blood pressure had their pressure drop almost immediately if a cat or dog was brought to their side or placed in their lap. People do reflexively pat companion animals when they come into contact with them, and patting seems to have an immensely calming effect on people suffering from hypertension. I don't believe all the science involved in this effect has been worked out. Whether the tactile sensation of fur on a warm body does it, whether the attention of another living creature does it, just isn't known, but there is more than enough evidence to suggest that Mesolithic man was on to something big, and even if statistics to support his actions and the science to explain it were ten to twenty thousand years in the future, he hung in there. How much of man's interest in the dog was based on some innate common sense cannot be told. More than utility was involved, much more. The bone record supports that. Of course, in the case of those early toys, affection could be considered a form of utility. We are just beginning to really understand another element in the man-dog bond, the psychological aspects, those that are strictly emotional. Studies have shown that people can be helped emotionally by dogs to an enormous degree. There have been some very graphic examples in my life and within my

view to bear out the critical nature this bond can assume.
I recognize it in myself and family, but I have seen it in a
very vivid way beyond my immediate intimate circle.

When I was fourteen years old, and large for my age, I got
a job at the famed Angell Memorial Animal Hospital.
Located on Longwood Avenue in the heart of Boston's vast,
sprawling medical district—Beth Israel, Boston Lying-in,
Boston Children's, Harvard Medical School, Mass. Dental,
and a host of other institutions were all within a few blocks
of Angell—it has been consistently rated one of the finest
veterinary hospitals in the world. It was operated then in its
old setting and is today in its new home on South Huntington Avenue by the Massachusetts Society for the Prevention
of Cruelty to Animals. The MSPCA is one of the oldest
humane societies in the western hemisphere.

The first assignment given to the eager and somewhat
brash new boy was, of course, cage cleaning. After my initial
trial period I graduated to the waist-high bathtubs in the
grooming section, watching my hands and forearms turn
into prunes as I worked. I bathed, clipped, and deburred
dogs all day long. I seriously questioned if my back would
ever be right again. A slight forward tilt for eight hours a
day can do one heck of a job, even on a teenager's sacroiliac.

Promotions came in proper order, and after passing
through some less rewarding departments (like the euthanasia room) I ended up in a white jacket in the clinic
helping the staff veterinarians, or at least doing menial
chores that made their lives a little easier. I hoisted animals
on and off examining tables (after first lathering the stain-
less-steel surfaces with antiseptic solutions), held animals
while they were examined and treated, guided clients in and
out, and took dogs and cats back and logged them in if they
had to be hospitalized. It was a rich experience for a boy just

turning fifteen. Heading for work after school and on weekends didn't seem a chore, really. I was beginning to focus
on a career. At that point I was determined to become a
veterinarian.

One day the veterinarian on duty groaned as he pulled a
card from the wooden holder on the wall. It was a familiar
card, one side completely filled in with very little room left
on the reverse.

"O.K., ask Mr. Jones to come in." (Jones was not his
name, but that hardly matters.)

The client was a tired man with gray skin. He gave the
impression that life had not been an unmixed blessing. His
weariness hung on him like an ill-fitting shawl. In his arms,
wrapped in an old but obviously frequently laundered blanket, was a positively ancient Boston terrier. The old man put
his old dog on the table gently, obviously with love, and
looked up at the tall young veterinarian, who towered over
him. There was some hope in the old man's eyes, a little, but
not really very much.

The veterinarian had seen this dog before, often, but he
went through the gestures of examining him: stethoscope
to heart, palpation of the abdomen, a look in the mouth and
down the throat, a quick glance in the ears.

"The new medicine doesn't seem to be helping very
much," the old man fairly croaked. "It's hard to tell, but
there doesn't seem to be much change."

The veterinarian looked down at the floor for a moment,
then put his foot on the rung of the examining table. He
took a deep breath and leaned forward, prepared to make
the speech he had made so many times before.

"You know there is never going to be any change, Mr.
Jones. You know very well I am giving you medication for
. . ." The veterinarian glanced over at the record card.

". . . for Gutsy to humor you. I can't be any blunter than that. Your dog is eighteen years old. He is blind, deaf, incontinent, he can't walk, he is frightened and in pain, and you are not being nice to him by keeping him alive this long. In nature he would have died long ago."

The young doctor was really being as kind as he knew how to be, but he had been begging Mr. Jones to have his dog put to sleep for over six months. Mr. Jones, however, was back every week trying new medication, always with the faintest hint of hope in his eyes. We all knew him. We all understood his plight, or at least we thought we did. There wasn't a veterinarian or a kennel helper at Angell who hadn't been through the same scene many times before.

"You don't think there is anything you can do?" The same question was asked every week.

"No, I *know* there is nothing we can do. We can't turn back the clock, and time has run out on Gutsy. You are not being kind to him by prolonging this very bad period for him."

The old man thought for a moment, then shook his head. He had come to a decision.

"Well, if it must be it must be. I'll take him home and do it now."

The veterinarian reached out and took the old man's elbow as he bent forward to wrap his old dog up and carry him away.

"Don't do that, please. It is a very difficult thing to do at home. You won't have the right materials, and you will be cruel to him even though you are trying to be kind. Let me do it here. I have a drug that will work very quickly. You can stay and help me if you want. You hold him and I will give him an injection. He won't even feel it and it will be over instantly. You will be able to see that for yourself. Please, don't try it yourself."

The old man thought again for a moment, then looked up into the veterinarian's eyes. Having finally decided to put his dog to death, the old man was finding new strengths, strengths that obviously had been eluding him for a long time.

"My wife died almost twenty years ago. I never wanted to remarry. We had just one son, and he married a girl in China. They have three children, but I have never been able to go there and they can't afford to come here. We're half a world apart. I don't know why God worked it out this way for me, but Gutsy is all the family I have had for a long, long time. If he has to be killed, I'll do it. It is up to me. Thank you, doctor."

The veterinarian started to protest again, but the old man had gathered his dog up in his arms and was at the door. I was in the process of opening it for him when he turned back.

"Gutsy and I really do appreciate everything you have tried to do. We understand, truly we do."

The old man was gone, and the doctor was shaking his head as he reached for the next card in the wall rack.

We read about it the next day. It wasn't front-page news, by any means, but it did make most of the Boston dailies. The old man had gone home, stuffed paper under the door, sealed the windows, and placed his rocking chair in front of the stove. He turned the oven on, but he didn't light it. I am sure he was rocking slowly, perhaps humming reassuringly to Gutsy, as they both went to sleep. I cried. I think the veterinarian did, too. I know some of the other kennel kids did, and I resented those who didn't.

The old man who committed suicide with his dog was not neurotic. He was an even-tempered, gentle, reasonable man whose one failing seemed to be his inability to let go of hope. Even when it was all stacked up against Gutsy he dared hope. Judging from the way he dealt with the veterinarians I saw him with, and with the kids who worked in the clinic, he was hardly a misanthrope. He was a nice old guy who had discovered, to his joy, the role a dog can play in a human life. His suicide was sad but understandable. He was not a "nut," he was not antisocial. He simply could not live with the inevitability of the truism that every pet taken into our lives is a tragedy waiting to happen.

Dr. Boris Levinson has been a pioneer in exploring the role of dogs in the lives of children. He has published two books on the subject, *Pet Oriented Child Psychotherapy* and *Pets and Human Development,* both published by Saunders. These professional publications are by no means the only studies done, for in this country as well as abroad the subject has been coming more and more under scrutiny.

The value of the bond between child and pet is based on a number of factors. There is again and perhaps in many cases foremost the matter of the pet's being nonjudgmental. Children are always under the gun to learn something, do something, become something, and they need constant approval. They seldom get enough. Kids are not always certain they are going to be able to live up to everyone's expectations of them. Many are frightened by what lies ahead, and why shouldn't they be? The most reliable source of approval for most youngsters is apparently a pet, and dogs are generally the most demonstrative of these. Kids can rely on their dogs to always pay attention to them, always approve of them, always find the time and energy to interact with them.

From the societal point of view, kids and dogs mix in another highly beneficial way. Kids are naturally egocentric and irresponsible. They react positively to whatever feels good and negatively to whatever does not. It takes some doing to bridge out of that hopeless mode and become a reliable social interactor. Dogs can help tremendously, because they can help responsibility and selflessness seem much less awesome. For many children, their first responsible actions, the first things they do on their own that are not for their own gratification, are in helping to care for a pet. Wise parents take advantage of this and encourage even tiny kids to check the water dish, and, in time, walk the dog. Certainly, kids can grow up to be responsible adults without having pets. It is just a whole lot easier, very often, if they do have them.

In Brewster, New York, there is a school for emotionally disturbed children called Green Chimneys. Approximately 40 percent of the students' time is spent on the school farm helping care for animals. Kids who had never been exposed to animals suddenly find themselves members of 4-H, find themselves going to the animals when they feel their own pressures building up inside. For many of them the farm at Green Chimneys is the first device other than drugs that has ever worked in getting themselves under control, keeping them from blowing up like volcanoes. Although dogs are not the focus at Green Chimneys, the point is still made. Children and animals are an incredibly healthy mix.

In Bridgeport, Connecticut, there is a home for alcoholics. I visited the institution and found that one of the keys to its program of rehabilitation was the dog, specifically the Labrador retriever. One patient-inmate of twenty-five sat cross-legged on his bed patting his Lab. He sobbed as he confessed to me he had been a skid-row bum since the age of sixteen. "This," he said, nodding toward his dog, "is the first responsibility I have ever accepted in my entire life without panicking." At a school called Lincoln Hall in northern Westchester County, New York, the brothers who ran the school for PINs (People in Need of Supervision; we used to call them juvenile delinquents) assigned different breeds of dogs to each of the bungalows. The twenty-four students and the dogs got along just fine, and the brothers felt the dogs helped enormously in rehabilitating the troubled youngsters.

The Lima State Institution in Lima, Ohio, houses men who have been classified as criminally insane. That is a kind of ultimate category. When you can't make it in a regular insane asylum, when even the penitentiaries don't want you, they send you to a place like Lima. The men arriving there have an attempted suicide rate of about 85 percent. Not only have many of the men tried to kill themselves one or more times, but many of them are self-mutilators. One of the men I interviewed had been kicked out of his former residence, the state penitentiary, because he had swallowed razor blades. There are six sections or wards in Lima where the men are allowed to keep pets. In seven years in those six sections there has not been one suicide attempt. This suggests that animals have a profound effect on mental health or at least on self-control. Where Valium failed in the other wards, pets succeeded in those assigned to them.

A specific event at Lima reveals how much animal companions can have to do with social control. One of the inmates went berserk in a recreation room. As so often happens with a group of people who are individually marginal in their social mechanisms, the insanity quickly spread. Men began beating each other up for no apparent reason, and then the room itself became the focus of their uncontrollable wrath. The television set was demolished. The curtains came down, the wood and glass windows disintegrated; only the steel bars beyond kept the explosion contained. Furniture sailed through the air; even a billiard table went down in splinters, although how that was accomplished without a bulldozer remains as much a mystery as the cause of the mayhem itself. When the orderlies and guards came pouring through the door and had wrestled the last inmate to the floor, only one thing remained standing amid a sea of rubble. Only the most fragile thing in the room was untouched—a fish tank.

The reaction of a group of frenzied criminal minds to a small colony of fragile tropical fish may not seem like a major reflection on man and dog, but it is. It shows again what happens when human beings and animals bond as the keepers and the kept, and what is involved in the companion animal.

There was a remarkable case in Holland related to me by one of the principals involved. He is an industrialist with factories and businesses all over the world. One of his enterprises is located in the extreme northern part of the Netherlands, sticking out into a cold, gray sea. The weather there is almost always dreadful, and people stay inside much of the time.

The man's business there is a large factory prefabricating concrete buildings, often entire settlements. He was awarded a contract for a U.S. Air Force base in Greenland. It was totally prefabricated at his plant, everything from barracks to chapel to mess hall to hangars and administration buildings. The base was shipped by sea.

His Dutch workers are models of skilled and semiskilled labor. He has never had labor trouble, and the enterprise has turned a substantial profit. He decided to declare a

bonus and called a workers' committee together to decide
how the bonus should be distributed. He offered them a
cash bonus, an improved insurance plan, a retirement plan,
what did they want? The committee said they would consult
with the men and report back.

Keep in mind that this was in a very desolate, remote area.
The men rode to work on bicycles carrying their lunches
with them. There was a long, gray, dull prefabricated dining
room where they gathered to get hot tea, chocolate, or
coffee and eat their lunches. It was where workers' meetings
were held, where all breaks were taken.

The committee reported back. The workers had agreed
—it had been unanimous—that they wanted the money
spent converting one long wall of their dining room into a
floor-to-ceiling aviary. They wanted green growing things
and birds. They wanted to be able to share their free time
with living creatures, things that would add color and life to
their gray world. They wanted to see birds from foreign
lands, things they could otherwise see only in books. They
wanted to be able not only to see and hear those feathered
creatures, they wanted to be able to care for them. And that
is how their bonus money was spent. My friend the industrialist was amazed but touched. He doesn't spend time at that
factory any more than he does at any of his others, but he
is somehow pleased that that beauty was asked for and
delivered as promised.

Again, birds on a peninsula in the North Sea are not dogs,
but the issue, the premise, is the same. Something good
happens inside people when they are able to cross a bridge
out of themselves into a more natural, less neurotic, and far
less demanding world beyond. Dogs remain the best or at
least the more popular of all the available bridges out-
bound.

Kate has been confined to a wheelchair all of her life. The daughter of a powerful, even awe-inspiring, and very beautiful author mother, Kate has had a great deal to contend with besides her own physical inadequacies. Fortunately, her mind is extremely acute and she is naturally sweet and generous. Kate needed something of her own. The parade of noted visitors her mother's fame brought through their handsome Victorian mansion was not enough, and neither were Kate's intense religious convictions. Not at all surprisingly, the answer was the old faithful companion. From her wheelchair Kate was able to obedience-train dogs and show them. Ribbons and trophies and framed photographs testify to more than twenty years of involvement, and dogs still grace the home and enrich the life of a woman who from the beginning seemed very, very short on luck. No one can even imagine how many hours those dogs filled and how desperately they were needed.

It is interesting and revealing that although fate decreed that Kate depend heavily on her dogs for companionship and fulfillment, she remains perhaps the least misanthropic human being I have ever known. No one is filled with more love or is more forgiving of her fellow humans' faults than Kate. The keeshonds, Newfoundlands, whippets, and German shepherds that have filled so many niches in Kate's life have in no way deprived her of her humanity. Except among the already desperately neurotic, dogs have the incredible capacity of remaining in their own emotional place. We need them, we may depend on them, but they never really replace people. It has been my experience that the opposite is true. Healthy dog lovers tend to be better people lovers than any dog haters I have ever known.

Dr. Samuel Corson and his wife and associate, Elizabeth O'Leary Corson, of Ohio State University's College of Medicine recently published a paper called "Pet Animals as Socializing Catalysts in Geriatrics: An Experiment in Non-verbal Communication Therapy." A premise is established early in the paper: "In industrial societies with high population mobility, the emotional trauma of economic and social isolation in the aged is often superimposed on an earlier layer of psychological stress associated with the 'empty nest syndrome.' " Further, the authors state: "The loss of economic and social roles induced by obligatory age-related retirement thus may accentuate the psychological stress of the empty nest syndrome and lead to loss of self-esteem and of the ability or willingness to maintain some semblance of independent functioning, socialization, and goal-directed activities." In a word, by life today old people are made to feel unwanted, useless, and therefore awfully lonely.

Having established their premise, the authors then go on to quote *Song of Myself* by Walt Whitman:

I think I could turn and live with animals, they
are so placid and self-contained,
I stand and look at them long and long.

They do not sweat and whine about their condition,
They do not lie awake in the dark and weep for their sins,
They do not make me sick discussing their duty to God,
Not one is dissatisfied, not one is demented with
the mania of owning things,
Not one kneels to another, nor to his kind that
lived thousands of years ago,
Not one is respectable or unhappy over the whole earth.

So they show their relations to me and I accept them,
They bring me tokens of myself, they evince them
plainly in their possession.

Armed with a premise and a rationale, they seek evidence of the value of dogs and other animals, although they do feel dogs make the best therapists. One aspect derives from the nonverbal signals health-care workers, doctors, nurses, attendants, and even friends and family send to the sick, the infirm, the disabled, and the mentally impaired. However hard we try not to do it we convey pity or disgust or concern or revulsion; in some way, generally through facial expressions and perhaps physical avoidance, we let less than perfect people know we find them if not repugnant then at least, well, less than perfect. That is apparently something that cannot be helped, because we usually don't know we are doing it. Dogs don't do that, and that fact can make the difference between sanity and near desperation in someone already beset by troubles.

The flow of negative signals apparently intensifies in the custodial setting, where the staff is inevitably overworked and the emotional needs of patients or residents overlooked. One way of breaking the cycle of negative signals that gives rise to increasing helplessness in a self-reinforcing circle is the introduction of attendants who can't participate—dogs, and to some extent other animals as well. Dogs are especially good because they are the most immediately and apparently responsive. (Not to be denied, however, is how well some cats can play the role.)

In addition to the nonjudgmental quality of dogs, there is another quality that works well for the elderly. Dogs maintain a kind of *perpetual infantile innocent dependence.* According to the Corsons, that stimulates in us a natural tendency to offer support and protection. It gives people a purpose, makes them not only feel wanted but *know* that they are wanted. It is not a game; no one has to pretend or patronize.

Dogs do need human support and show gratitude when they get it.

All that brings us to another quality in the dog that makes it so endearing. Although the dog plays a role, it is not a conscious role player. A dog is utterly sincere. It cannot pretend, it cannot act in any way patronizing no matter how physically or emotionally incapacitated the human partici- pant is. For a dog every human being is exactly the same, except some are more responsive and likable, from the dog's point of view, than others.

The fact that people do not have to be suspicious of a dog's reactions to them is in itself an enormous measure of potential mental health. You may question almost all or perhaps all of the people in your life, but you don't question your dog. People use you and pretend they don't, while dogs use you in complete honesty because they have no choice, and they have not an ounce of deceit in their soul nor self-consciousness about any of this. It is certainly true that dogs have been symbols of evil and in mythology have played a wide variety of roles, but on a one-to-one basis they are not suspect, and old people, frightened people, alien- ated people, and people alone for whatever reason are fre- quently suspicious. To be able to relate without having to doubt, to be able to love or even just like a whole lot without having to fear rejection, is a source of comfort more fortu- nate people cannot begin to imagine. We can't, after all, imagine a toothache, not really; and we certainly can't imag- ine the terrors of lurking paranoia. A dog may be a nice pal to you, but it may be utter salvation for someone less fortu- nate.

Few if any of these factors could have been known to the people who first socialized *Canis lupus pallipes,* but then little was known to them about vitamins, proteins, and carbohydrates, yet they knew how to eat. Even people who do not understand the biological connection between sexual intercourse and pregnancy still engage in sexual intercourse, because nature, anticipating the essential nature of the act if the species was to survive, made the act pleasurable and therefore automatically repeatable whatever the biological sophistication of the participants. People have sex because it feels good, they eat because it feels good, and for a very long time they have kept companion animals because it feels good. The intellectualization of all three came long after the invention.

Without doubt the ways in which human beings bond to nonhuman creatures will be under investigation for decades. Ph.D.s will be awarded to the investigators by the score, and that is all to the good. The status of the dog and of all companion animals can only be raised by such studies, and that will come at a time when dogs and other animals, wild and domestic, can use all the help they can get. Without doubt, adults and children will benefit, because controlled programs using animals can have remarkably beneficial effects. In the complex world of the man-dog interface, things are looking up.

4
Diversity I: The Sporting, Hound, and Working Dogs

One of the things that allow dogs to fit into our lives—and us into theirs—is their incredible diversity. Compared to an aquarium of marine fish or a zoo aviary, dogs are not diverse. There is one big, marvelous difference, however. The fish and the birds are of many species; dogs all belong to one. The ostrich and the hummingbird come down to us on altogether different tracks through time. The chihuahua and the St. Bernard sprang from the same historical loins, so to speak. There is no other animal under our control that is so elastic, and no counterpart is known in nature. Man and nature have obviously conspired to stretch one set of genes about as far as any known set. Man has been the beneficiary.

If you took a St. Bernard, a cocker spaniel, a coyote, a timber wolf, a bloodhound, a toy Manchester terrier, and any other sixteen breeds of dogs you might care to select and put them all in a big pen you could come back in perhaps a dozen years or so and find a very familiar dog in their midst, their common descendant. You would look and say, "Thy name is dog." On the loose, dog genes all end up heading in the same direction. The first few generations into the experiment would not reveal this. The retracing of their own evolution would be a function of time. But it would happen unerringly.

I have seen that ubiquitous, universal dog in Sri Lanka, India, Thailand, Korea, Japan, Pakistan, and Bangladesh. I have seen that dog in Turkmenistan in Central Soviet Asia and in Russia, in Kenya, Tanzania, Angola, Mozambique, Liberia, Senegal, Egypt, Portugal, England, Mexico, Canada, New Zealand, Australia, the Netherlands, and all over the United States. It usually has prick or upstanding ears. It has a rather snipey snout, a bit bitchy in fact. It has a gray to brown coat (sort of medium mouse), dainty feet, minimal dewclaws (which appear in the dog but not in the wolf), and a somewhat brushy tail that may curve out and down or possibly up and over, the latter feature, up and over, revealing northern spitz influence. The adult dog will probably weigh between thirty and forty pounds and have light bones and a small head. That seems to be what dogs go toward on their own with no one overseeing their sex lives. It could be a clue, because that general description does point in the direction of a small wolf, except for the curved tail that seems to linger on in a lot of dogs and that is definitely not wolfish.

We prefer not to let dogs breed out of control, of course; we style them, sculpt them, design them, and breed for the idealized standards we set. It is a sport, an art, a science, and a pleasure. It is because we can style them to taste, color them to style, and order them down to the fine details that dogs serve our egos so well. They are extensions of us. When you can have them big and small, skinny and fat, push-faced or aquiline, klutzy or as graceful as a tern, short-haired and long-haired, as athletic as a ballet dancer or as sedentary as, well, a bulldog, you really can have it your way. It can also be more complicated than buying a new car, there are so many options. In order to handle the incredible variability in dogs we divide the officially recognized breeds in the United States into seven groups.

Before outlining the groups I should clarify some terms. There is much to be said for speaking a common language. There is no such thing as a *thoroughbred* dog. A Thoroughbred is a specific breed of horse and in no context is the term properly applied to a canine. There, I have said it, but half of America will still go around speaking of their thoroughbred poodle, Spot. We use *purebred* and *full-bred* interchangeably, although some zealots spend their lives trying to convince anyone who will listen that *full-bred* is the only acceptable term. Personally, I remain unconvinced. The counterpoint to purebred or full-bred is the so-called mongrel. All manner of less than amusing names are applied to these dogs—mongrels, mutts, pooches, and, for some reason, Heinz. The fact that Mr. Heinz made fifty-seven different kinds of condiments from cucumbers and tomatoes somehow convulses people when it is applied to a dog of apparently relaxed lineage. I stared blankly the first time I heard the hilarious comparison implied, and I stare just as blankly now, forty-odd years later. The likening of a twenty-thousand-year-old friend to chutney or a sweet gherkin just doesn't do it for me. As a Japanese friend of mine would put it, "No ding-dong inside." I do, however, have a preferred name for dogs of universal descent. I call them *random-breds*, and, with appropriate dignity, that seems to stand as a neat counterpoint to a full-bred or purebred. I think dignity for the not-so-purebred dog is a worthwhile pursuit.

The group generally listed as number one, although with no particular logic, is the Sporting Group. There are some inconsistencies in its membership, as there are in all the groups, but twenty-four breeds are designated as sporting dogs today. They are all of European origin, the majority from Germany, Spain, and the British Isles. A few were refined in the United States from European stocks. The sporting dogs listed by the American Kennel Club are:

Pointer	Spaniel, Brittany
Pointer, German	Spaniel, Clumber
Shorthair	Spaniel, Cocker
Pointer, German Wirehair	Spaniel, English Cocker
Retriever, Chesapeake Bay	Spaniel, English Springer
Retriever, Curly-Coated	Spaniel, Field
Retriever, Flat-Coated	Spaniel, Irish Water
Retriever, Golden	Spaniel, Sussex
Retriever, Labrador	Spaniel, Welsh Springer
Setter, English	Vizsla
Setter, Gordon	Weimaraner
Setter, Irish	Wirehaired Pointing
Spaniel, American Water	Griffon

In the sporting group there is one breed from the Netherlands, the wirehaired pointing griffon, one from Hungary, the vizsla, and several from Germany—the weimaraner and the German wirehaired and shorthaired pointers. Those developed to some extent in North America are the Chesapeake Bay retriever, the Labrador retriever (which came from Newfoundland, not Labrador, and which was developed in its present form in British kennels), and the American water spaniel. There was so much exchange way back, however, with the setter and the pointer stock coming from the Iberian Peninsula, that nation of origin frequently means a good deal less than most people would have us believe. The Brittany spaniel was a continental develop-ment, for instance, arising largely in France, but it too was of probable Spanish stock and shouldn't even be called a spaniel at all. It is much more of a setter in size and field performance.

There is an unmistakable panache to the sporting dogs, and that is understandable. It isn't by accident that they have little or no Asian or African influence in them. They have been the dogs of common people with leisure. It is certainly true that people have taken out their hunting dogs to get meat needed for their table, but far more often the sporting dog has been part of a game people have played, a kind of recreational killing. People who are into field sports very often have a style of their own—the right after-shave, the right boots, jackets, and other paraphernalia, not to mention pipe tobacco. Part of that paraphernalia has been a dandy-looking, high-stepping dog. Since field dogs have been expected to do certain specific things, breeders of dogs in this group have been rather less tolerant than breeders of less purpose-oriented breeds. A pointer has to point and a retriever has to retrieve, and there are right and wrong ways of doing both.

The performance demanded of the real field dog is as tightly tied into the animal's genes as its coat color, length of leg, and depth of brisket. Very often the poor animal does things without even knowing why except for a nagging from somewhere in its cells that says, *Do it, boy, do it or else.* We have a lovely golden retriever named Jeremy Boob in our menagerie. He simply has to retrieve or burst. When company arrives he frantically races around looking for a retrieving job, knowing instinctively that that is what he was born to do and, not incidentally, it is one guaranteed way of gaining approval. Most guests walk up the front steps to find Jeremy standing there wagging his tail with a cushion or pillow in his mouth. He drops the pillow on command and waits to be congratulated on yet another great save. He has been retrieving pillows since he was a puppy, and it is a habit that is impossible to break. Indeed, why would one want to break it and deny Jerry his purpose in being? Since we don't shoot birds around our place he has to express his ability to retrieve in some way. As for walking back down the drive from the mailbox, heaven help you if Jeremy can't carry at least the third-class mail.

Retrievers have a remarkable built-in computing system that is tied to what may be close to being the best eyesight in the dog world. You can take Jeremy out on the beach behind our house and throw a stick. It doesn't matter how high or how far you throw it, and if there is any daylight left at all. Jeremy is under this stick when it comes down. He handles parabolas, altitudes, speed, and EPI (expected point of impact) like a multi-eyed computerized machine. If he could hit, the ball clubs would be after him. Retrievers are incredible outfielders.

Jeremy's fielding ability led to a strange confrontation a few years back. Six-month-old Yankee, a perfectly splendid bloodhound puppy, joined us in 1975. Jeremy was already mature, and Yankee accepted, as his genes insisted he must, the dominant male already in place. But since Jeremy was a retriever, Yankee assumed he must be, too. They were exercised together along with several of the other dogs, and Yankee pounded on down the beach with the best of them after the airborne stick. Problem, though: A bloodhound can't see beans in a pan. They don't have to, since they can smell a single bean a mile away. Yankee was never under the stick when it came down except by accident, and then it was usually to have it land on his head. Jeremy's elegant midair pirouettes to snatch the stick a few feet before impact were simply not in the bloodhound repertoire. A lost stick in heavy growth was a cinch for Yankee to find by smell, but not when it was sailing overhead.

But time plays tricks on all of us, and the trick it played on Jeremy was in the form of a submissive puppy that wouldn't stop growing. At eight months Yankee, the flop-eared klutz, was bigger than Jeremy, and at ten months he was pushy. The time finally came when Jeremy would catch the stick and Yankee would tug it away from him and run to home base for the reward, leaving the poor air dancer Jeremy standing looking dejected and cheated, which, indeed, he had been.

Ah, but all that breeding for guaranteed performance in the field was not for naught. Jeremy finally outwitted Yankee. He would pound on down the flat and catch the stick with his usually superb elevation, twist and snatch, and then immediately head for the nearest beach plum. Up went the leg and the letter was mailed. Yankee, a male, too, of course, would come bounding along intent on stealing the stick and the thunder when he would encounter Jeremy in the act of marking that bush. Some things in a dog rise above even the desire to gain praise. Yankee had absolutely no choice. A male had sent a message, and he, as a male, had to answer it. Waiting his turn, he would mark on top of Jeremy's mark while Jeremy shot back to headquarters with the prize. Poor Yankee was locked into place. He stood there helpless, peeing with the silliest look on his face as he lost out time and again. Jeremy was triumphant. Wondrously they are still very good friends today, long after the stick throwing has stopped. Yankee has a heart condition and Jeremy's hips hurt him, so they spend most of their time, I guess, remembering. (I am not absolutely certain of this, but it seems to me that once Jeremy had worked out his keep-the-stick technique he would take a long drink of water just before an exercise session.)

The most popular dog in America in the Sporting Group doesn't even belong in the group in the opinion of some people. It is the cocker spaniel, a breed that has been reduced in size and jaw length so much, and so heavily burdened with decorative fur or feathers or *furniture,* that most of them could no longer function in the field except in very structured events. As we will be seeing, the sixth group is called the Nonsporting Group. Today it is a perfectly meaningless name. That group could be renamed the Companion Group and should probably include the cocker. The English cocker, from which our cocker is descended, was designated English cocker in this country in 1946. The American version of the cocker and that English cocker really are two very different dogs today. The back-and-forth nature of dog-breed designation is well illustrated by the spaniels.

Up until the seventeenth century the spaniels were undifferentiated. They were dogs of Spain and came small and large, fast and slow. They were the land spaniels that had already been separated from the somewhat larger setters. Some of the larger spaniels excelled at springing or scaring up a variety of game, and some of the smaller varieties excelled at work on woodcock. This became so pronounced that in 1892 the Kennel Club in England recognized them as breeds, the springer spaniel and the cocking or cocker spaniel. That cocker was to become in time what we call today the English cocker.

Up until 1892 what we now call the English cocker and the springer spaniels could appear in the same litter. There was no real difference except in size and the work to which they were put in the field.

There was a parallel development in progress. The basic field spaniel was evolving, the line that later would give rise to the Sussex, springer, field, and cocker spaniel. But there was a smaller, push-faced spaniel with a round head and a predominantly red-and-white coat often called the Marl-borough spaniel or the Marlborough cocker. In time it became the English toy spaniel. It is listed today in the Toy Group. It is a cuddly little creature and is supposed to be spoiled rotten. That is its function. The English toy spaniels pout superbly, about as well as good retrievers retrieve. Some of the Marlboroughs were crossed with the smaller field spaniels, and the cocker that America was soon to import with great enthusiasm emerged. The cocker spaniel favored here (it was smaller and tended to have a rounder head) was not distinguished from the really very different cocker favored in England (that had had very little Marlborough spaniel influence) until the middle 1930s. Then it was that fanciers of the English version of the cocker pressed successfully for their own breed recognition. The English cocker spaniel and the cocker spaniel are very different animals today. Each, though, is a sculptured work of art and when properly maintained can hold its own in any hearty contest. No longer real winners on the gaming grounds, they are triumphant in the drawing room. (In all fairness some breeders do still produce cockers and English cockers for field competition. They are in the minority.)

The weimaraner, one of Germany's top sporting dogs, dates back less than two hundred years. It was meticulously developed by noble sporting patrons at the court of Wei-

mar. It was a snob sporting dog developed and jealously
guarded by one of the biggest collection of snobs the dog
world has ever seen. You were *right* or you couldn't get your
hands on one. Bloodhound stock clearly played a large role
at the beginning, as did a German breed not known in this
country, the red schweisshund. The weimaraner is a first
cousin to the German shorthaired pointer.

The weimaraner is a perfect example of a highly refined
breeding experiment that paid off, but it did produce a
breed that is exactly right for some kinds of people and
perfectly dreadful for others. The snobs of Weimar weren't
entirely wrong in the degree to which they protected their
creation.

The solid mouse to silver-gray weimaraner with its short,
dense coat is a dog that simply must have early obedience
training or it is capable of being a first-class pest. It is
headstrong, willful, adoring, incredibly intelligent, and responsive to praise. When a weimaraner doesn't know what
it is supposed to do it can be counted on to do all the wrong
things. I have known weimaraners whose owners had not
bothered to train them or teach them manners to go
through a plate-glass picture window because they had been
left home alone too long and were bored, bless them. I
knew of one that dragged a charred log from a fireplace and
pulled it from room to room chewing charcoal off it as it
went. It took a professional cleaning firm to repair the damage. It could have burned the house down.

That kind of flaky behavior must be seen in contrast to the
well-managed dog, however, or it gives a distorted picture.
A well-trained weimaraner is a regal accomplishment of
canine genetic art, and as intolerably ill-behaved as a mis-
managed specimen can be, that is how extremely good,
solid, and reliable a properly raised example will be. It is

one of those dogs, and this is so often true of the sporting dogs, that is what you want it to be. Few dogs can be more of a nuisance than an Irish setter, a vizsla, or a weimaraner that has had its vital energy levels, its need to perform, and its exuberant affair with life ignored. They need exercise, they need training, and they need opportunities to participate in vigorous, ongoing events. You ignore those facts at considerable risk to your property. I have known very few sporting dogs that had anything at all wrong with them except their owners.

But not all breeds are as easy to trace to their source. Well over a thousand years ago, hordes of Magyars swept into what is now Hungary. They engaged in field sports, we know, including such refined activities as falconry. Drawings from the tenth century reveal sporting noblemen, and they often seem to be accompanied by a dog that looks very much like the vizsla. It was quite probably just about the same short-haired, distinctively solid rusty gold to dark sandy yellow dog we know today, but tracing its origins back further than that would be impossible. What role the sleek, athletic vizsla may have played in the development of the other quick-witted field dogs of middle Europe is also impossible to determine. There may be vizsla blood in the weimaraner, in any or all of the pointing breeds, but no one can say. The history of the dog for the last thousand years is often as cloudy as its history during the ten to fifteen thousand years before that. One of the problems, of course, is that we have lost the intermediate forms and ten centuries ago there was far less note-taking than today and no photography. Not only did people not have cameras, most of them couldn't write. If the Magyars kept a stud book on the vizsla it hasn't turned up. What is more important, however, is that they kept their lines pure. Considering the chaos in

Europe during the last ten centuries the fact that a dog was held in pure form is something that is, at the very least, remarkable. The Crusades came and went, the Dark Ages flowed across peoples and international boundaries, creating a cloud of universal fear and ignorance, plagues killed a third of the population at a time, wars that we can no longer even identify tore kingdoms and dukedoms and entire civilizations apart, but the vizsla hung in there. In spite of terror, disease, appalling ignorance, ill will, and drunken orgies of power and shifting loyalties, some breeders somewhere managed to keep their line of dogs pure. It must have been terribly important to them. It probably cost some their fortunes, possibly some their lives.

That apparently dramatic last assertion is justified because we do know of times and places in history when it was against the law for anyone but royalty to own certain select breeds. Dogs have been used as ransom, dogs have been taxable property, dogs have marked people as members of definite classes, and in hard times, like those in the Middle Ages, that could have been dangerous. The keeshond was a dangerous political liability in Holland, if the Prince of Orange's undercover men caught you with one. In China anyone attempting to own breeds reserved for the emperor and his favorite concubines was executed, so the stories go. There have been times when dog-owning was not as simple and as safe as it is now. The good old days weren't always that good.

The Brittany spaniel is another breed with a remarkable history and one that has been fairly well pieced together, although it still contains a healthy ratio of conjecture. Like the other spaniels, the setters, and the pointers, the original stock was almost certainly Iberian. Just when the bloodline was carried north from Spain (or Portugal) is not known, but it was a long time ago. Some of that stock remained on the Continent, although most moved across the Channel to England, where the bulk of field-dog development was to take place. Many people feel that the Brittany spaniel of today is related to the Irish setter. That breed is known to us as a splendid mahogany beast, but originally it was red and white. The Brittany is liver or orange and white. Early in the fifth century, Irish military chieftains invaded Gaul, now France. They almost certainly brought hunting dogs with them, and some of those may have figured in the strain that was to become the Brittany spaniel.

There is a language clue that may lend support to that conjecture. There is another spaniel in France that is orange and white and known as the *épagneul écossais* or Scotch spaniel. At the time of the Irish invasions, the Irish were known as Scoti.

Our Brittany today is tailless, or nearly so. That form does not comply, of course, with the Irish-setter look. It is a development less than a century old. The ancestors of the abbreviated-tail form appeared in the town of Pontou in the Douron Valley. A bitch that was mahogany and white, like the old Irish setter, and a lemon-and-white field dog brought to the region by an Englishman looking for woodcock were introduced. They bred, and two of their puppies were tailless. One of the two was apparently superior in the field, and it was kept as a stud. A percentage of every litter he sired had his bobbed profile.

The Brittany is an interesting character, but again it is a field dog first and certainly foremost. It needs exercise, it needs an assignment, it needs to work. It is not a specialized field dog, but one of great intensity, and that is reflected at home at the end of the day. Brittanies are assertive animals, devoted, seemingly dour or at least uninterested, very often, in strangers, but sportsmen all the way. They want to get out there and find game, and they want that game brought down. They perform perfectly well as retrievers. They are enormously popular in this country as well as abroad, and that must mean they are the pet an awful lot of people are looking for.

Some years ago a house guest arrived and unexpectedly brought her favorite Brittany with her. I don't know why people assume that since you have a dozen or so dogs yourself one more won't throw you. They are wrong. One more will throw you if it is not an easily acclimated animal. This particular Brittany was not, at least at the outset. It nearly went wild with joy when confronted with ten cats. In no time at all it had a cat arched, hissing and glowering, from the shoulders of everyone in the room. They retreated leaving claw marks on the way up. There is nothing worse than having an angry, frightened cat using you for a tree with a delightfully game and happy Brittany doing a combination Spanish jig and Irish reel around your legs.

When every cat had had its nervous breakdown, a few minutes' work, the resident dogs were next. Within moments they were all glowering and muttering under their breath. Satisfied that it had made its entrance noticed, the Brittany flopped on its side to hyperventilate a bit and reregulate its chemistry and temperature. It had all been very strenuous.

The performance was repeated several times before one of our dogs, I have forgotten which one, finally got up, stretched, and nailed the Brittany to the floor with a lionlike roar. Threatened with having its throat torn out, the Brittany settled down for the rest of the weekend and was a perfectly pleasant dog to have around. The cats generally stayed high for the two days and our dogs kept throwing us soul-destroying looks (I think they thought the Brittany was a permanent addition), but it worked out well. But that is the Brittany for you. It goes into every situation with a marked degree of enthusiasm. Game for the game, as we say.

There are twenty breeds in the hound group today. They are listed as follows:

Afghan Hound	Greyhound
Basenji	Harrier
Basset Hound	Ibizan Hound
Beagle	Irish Wolfhound
Black and Tan Coonhound	Norwegian Elkhound
Bloodhound	Otter Hound
Borzoi	Rhodesian Ridgeback
Dachshund	Saluki
Foxhound, American	Scottish Deerhound
Foxhound, English	Whippet

And what a diverse collection that is. It contains the tallest dog in the world, the Irish wolfhound, and a few other giants as well. The Scottish deerhound with an awful lot of leg under it is one of the tallest of dogs, and the borzoi (until 1936 called the Russian wolfhound) and the bloodhound are big animals. The hounds, with notable exceptions like that animated peapod the dachshund, the absolutely irresistible basset, and the wonderful whippet, may not be everybody's cup of tea, or dog. Although they are not listed as sporting dogs, of course, most hounds are exactly that. They are hunting equipment. The big coursing breeds, from greyhound on up to the giants we have already indicated, have wicked jaws that can cut a cat's or rabbit's spine in half in a midair snap. The coursing hounds are fast, have incredible eyesight, and take killing very seriously.

The pack hounds—beagles, foxhounds, harriers, and to some extent otterhounds—also take the pursuit of game very seriously. There is a major difference between the hunting hounds (which is most hounds) and the sporting dogs. The sporting dogs facilitate man's killing of animals with guns or other weapons. The hounds are the weapons themselves. A notable exception, as we will be seeing, is the bloodhound. It is used to track man but never to attack him.

The great giants among the hounds, like so many giant dogs, are subject to a very unfortunate condition known as timidity. It is by no means universal, but it is widespread and should be checked for and avoided. There is nothing sadder than an Irish wolfhound that is literally terrified by its own shadow. We have friends with a handsome wolfhound bitch named Olivia who lives in constant fear of everything that moves, doesn't move, might move, or could possibly stand still. It appears from the outside looking in (which is just about the only access we have to a dog's mind) that it is a life of real pain. If ever the expression "hangdog" had meaning it applies to the great hulk of a dog afraid of a canary singing and turned to jelly by a ringing doorbell. It does not apply to the slobber-jowled, long-eared blood-hound-basset look.

The local police in our town had a resident basset until a strange car passing through the village ended its career. And what was that career, you ask? Harassing the mailman. At the same time every day the mailman would pass the police station, sometimes on tiptoes, on one occasion wearing a false beard. (No false beard ever fooled a basset hound's nose.) No matter what he did, the mailman had to traverse that block followed by a baying basset who never, ever tried to bite him, but insisted on singing him on his way. Shopkeepers and customers alike gathered at the doors of all the stores along the way to watch or perhaps listen to the performance. The poor mailman was always red-faced, especially if it was during the tourist season and there were strangers in town. He would try crossing the street, but that didn't get the mail delivered on the basset's side, and besides, the basset would simply cross over and continue the performance. It was during one of the cross-overs that the basset came to his end. The mailman admit-ted how much he missed the old pest. It had been a fine if noisy understanding. The police now have a bloodhound named Jerusha, nicknamed Roo. The basset's daily routine was typical of the breed. A hound with an idea is almost immovable. They are very conservative souls. They like to do things in the same way every day.

Whippets are, of course, sight hounds. Their nose counts for little, their eyes for all. But they are no less stubborn than the big-nosed hounds. A whippet, for instance, knows that it should not feel cold. You have two choices: you can provide it with a blanket that the whippet can roll itself into whenever it wants to, or you can make your beds several times a day, or at least a favored bed. We once gave a whippet to a friend as a gift, and the dog took no time at all in making its demand understood: a blanket available, as available as water for ad-lib use, or down come the spreads. A whippet knows how and where to get warm. Don't deny it. It doesn't have all that much meat on its bones. One of the most delightful and beautiful of all dogs, the whippet, except for its dislike of the cold, is one of the finest of our pet breeds.

The hounds are quite likely the oldest purebreds still with

us. The afghan, the first hound on the list, probably dates back to the Sinai Peninsula six thousand years ago. At least there is a papyrus document that puts it there at about that time. A thousand years earlier than that there was a dog that bears a striking resemblance to the saluki in Sumeria. It was certainly around in its present form when Alexander the Great invaded India in 329 B.C. And the greyhound can be traced to the valley of the Nile as far back as 5,900 years ago, to the Fourth Dynasty, and is probably even more venerable than that. The ibizan hound is probably no younger as a breed.

It is interesting but hardly surprising that the oldest surviving breeds that have retained their original form are coursing hounds, high-speed animals with wicked, punishing jaws that ran game to earth for their masters. Gazelle, rabbit, even things like leopards were run and killed by packs of swift dogs with thin, graceful legs and enormous chests giving them the added lung capacity that kind of work requires. Domestic animals, particularly horses and dogs, have greater stamina than their wild counterparts. Stamina was what early hunters bred into their coursing hounds, that and light bones and virtually fat-free bodies.

There are four hounds that I personally consider misplaced in the Hound Group. The basenji, the handsome seventeen-inch, twenty-four-pound yodeling dog (they don't, of course, really bark) from Africa, is of unknown origin. Again, the sixth group now called the Nonsporting Group should be called the Companion Dog Group, and that is where the basenji might logically fit in. Heaven alone knows how much hound blood went into the basenji a couple of thousand years ago in Central Africa or Egypt, but we certainly don't know it as a hound and we have never used it to do a hound's work here or in Europe.

The origin of the basenji has been the subject of a great deal of scholarship both good and bad. Efforts have been made to trace a path through an incredible tangle of African linguistic stocks to see who may have had the dog, where and when. Relationships of ancient cultures without written records and without real records of the languages then in use (languages, like dodos and dinosaurs, are subject to extinction, by natural causes like the dinosaurs or because of man's destructiveness like the dodo) are very difficult to establish.

Rock carvings, rock paintings, traditional knowledge, symbology, legendry, all have been examined, but to no avail. The basenji may have originated as a domestic breed on the West Coast of Africa (not terribly likely), in Egypt (strong possibility), or in the Congo (certainly possible). There is no doubt that it moved back and forth between those regions with the tides of man. There were political migrations, movements of conquest (as there always have been in Africa), migrations because of disease, famine, and desertification, and, of course, trade. In this vast uncharted, unremembered pulse and flow there was a small, prick-eyed, curly-tailed dog which, for some reason, was bred to yodel and chortle, not to bark. The breed has other characteristics as well, including a penchant for sanitization. Basenjis wash themselves more meticulously than other dogs, rather like cats, in fact. They have a characteristic way of attracting attention, a sweeping movement of the paw from the ear down off the tip of the nose. All of these things are characteristic of the breed, and all make the basenji of uncertain origin, but none of them makes the basenji a hound.

The basenji *may* be between five thousand and eight thousand years old. It *may* be on a line with the oldest breeds known. It *may* have common ancestry with the ancient coursing hounds, pharaoh, saluki, greyhound, ibizan, but it is well removed from those powerful coursers, and to think of it today as a hound does not really seem to make too much sense in my opinion.

The occasional suggestion here that a dog be moved from one group to another is not to deny history (the poodle was a water retriever, but is no longer a sporting dog; the akita was used for hunting, as was the bloodhound, but they are not sporting dogs; and there are a score of other examples), nor does it diminish the stature of a breed. Realignment has only one purpose, and it is the same purpose we find in the breed lineup we have. The idea is to place dogs in groups that make showing them as nearly logical as possible.

The dachshund is a breed that looks a wee bit silly next to a Scottish deerhound or bloodhound. The word *Hund* does not mean "hound" in German, it means "dog," and *Dachs* means "badger." As far back as the fifteenth century there were hunting dogs in use in Europe that were bred for tenacity and short legs. They went to earth after everything from rabbit to badger, and from that line the dachshund we know now almost certainly came. Larger dachshunds than we are familiar with are still used in Europe in the field. They come in three coat and several color varieties, and there are miniature dachshunds of each variety that weigh under ten pounds. The original mixture that created the old dachshund included hound almost certainly, but it also included terrier. Old illustrations aren't reliable, but they do show short legs on a dog with a terrier head. I have one woodcut in my collection that dates to 1636, and the dog was no more a hound than a terrier then. The dachshund, at least in the United States, is a companion dog today and belongs in neither the Hound Group nor the Terrier Group, but rather in the proposed Companion Dog Group.

The Norwegian elkhound is a magnificent working animal with a horrendously shrill bark that carries well at night. It was a hunter and a guard and companion of Vikings between five and six thousand years ago. It is a northern spitz breed, and grouping it away from the northern sled dogs in the Working Group is strange to say the least. Why doesn't it belong with the keeshond, which is in the Non-sporting Group? All of the heavy-coated northern spitzes belong together.

The elkhound (it was, we assume, used to hunt the elk, which is what the Scandinavians call the moose) is not known to everyone in the United States. That is something of a shame, but it is true of a lot of breeds. I knew one couple who bought an elkhound in a pet shop (which is something no one should ever do, for reasons I will explain later in this book) and were told it was a "miniature husky," a particularly rare breed. It certainly is rare, so rare in fact that this dog was the only known example. Undeterred, these slightly known neighbors lived for years with their "mini-husky" and boasted of it to everyone they could get to listen. Those of us who knew the truth got tired of telling them, and the neighbors who didn't know were variously intrigued or bored. At a thousand curb and hydrant stops the story was repeated. This rarest of rare dogs with his doting owners finally moved away to begin the legend anew at some new hydrants in a different city. In the meantime, not the least disturbed by the controversy that had its foundation in his very being, Old Minihusk was one heck of a watchdog and an all-around great pet. They kept him well brushed, and obviously his diet was just right, and I suspect all that was far more important than his real identity. Still, it seems a shame to ignore a history as intriguing and full of adventure as the Norwegian elkhound's. It stood in the

prow of many a Viking boat, warned of the approach of a
lot of bears and armed invaders, helped explore a new
world, and did, I am sure, help hunt the largest member of
the deer family. Miniature huskies have nowhere near as
exciting a history!

The fourth question mark in the hound group, the
Rhodesian ridgeback, was bred out of European imports in
southern Africa. The international mix included great
danes, mastiffs, greyhounds, terriers, bloodhounds, and a
variety of pointer, spaniel, and setter types, all mixed with
a native African dog we know only as the hottentot dog.
That African animal came from heaven alone knows where,
heaven alone knows when. All of these animals were undoubtedly blended between the sixteenth and eighteenth
centuries. Now why, after all of that breeding, for which
there are no records, we should call the Rhodesian ridgeback a hound is beyond me. There is hound in the golden
retriever, too, in all likelihood.

The archetypical scent hound is the bloodhound. Cynolo-
gists are not certain where or when the breed evolved into
its present form, but it is quite probably true that the breed
with its unbelievable nose was found along the northern
Mediterranean coastline before the birth of Christ. They
certainly were around before the Crusades and were known
in Constantinople. It is likely that there were both black and
white varieties in the early days, and it is believed that the
black version gave rise to what has been known in France
as St. Hubert's hound since the eighth or ninth century.
Strains were developed in France and England, and both
figured prominently in the construction of many of our
modern breeds, particularly some of our sporting breeds
that were compelled by their field assignments to have good
noses.

How did such a placid beast—for the bloodhound is as gentle as a dog can be—get such a dreadful name? As always, there are a good many stories that include a mythical bloodthirsty nature. Pure rot! The suggestion as to the origin of the name "bloodhound" that I think most probably accurate dates back to the Middle Ages. There are said to have been two classes of hounds then in vogue. One was a rather coarse dog of medium talents. It was available to the common man. It was everyman's hound. Then there was an exquisitely refined scenting hound that was restricted in ownership to titled people and the royal family; it was the hound of the blood (meaning blueblood) or the blooded hound. It had nothing at all to do with sanguinary propensities; it was just an indication of its quality and the restrictions on its ownership. It was not far from hound-of-the-blood or blooded-hound to bloodhound.

The motion-picture industry has had a field day with the bloodhound for years. They usually present the dog just about 180 degrees off the mark. Everyone has seen the familiar sequence of the escaped convict bashing his way through swamps with yowling hounds in hot pursuit. Terrific stuff. White knuckles in the audience. The question is, will he be zapped by a rattlesnake or eaten by the dogs first or will he take his own life in desperation? Strong stuff, all right, but let's look at the bloodhound on the trail as he actually is. For trailing bloodhounds are in fact a part of modern police work, even if they are transported and guided by helicopters. They are like infantrymen in combat. Sooner or later someone has to get down on the ground and slug it out.

The bloodhound trails silently. It does not go roaring through the woods like a sound-effects department gone berserk. If you were trailing a criminal you suspected might be armed, would you want your dog announcing your arrival in advance? Bloodhounds are not used in packs. Rarely two dogs will be trailed together, but it is usually the single dog that makes the find. Bloodhounds are never trailed off lead, for several reasons. They have no road sense, and if indeed they did come to a highway they would never lift their heads off the scent trail. A free-running bloodhound is sooner or later, and frequently sooner, a dead dog. And since the record trail run by a bloodhound was 138 miles (with relays of handlers, of course), the bloodhound off the lead might never be seen again. When they dig in and go with those powerful hindquarters (a bloodhound can weigh over 150 pounds—they are not oversized beagles, as so many people picture them) they *go* and would be quickly gone, probably for good.

But all of the other mistakes in the Hollywood image of the noble bloodhound pale before the idea, the mere suggestion, that the great sniffers attack their quarry. They kiss them. By far the largest percentage of the bloodhound courses run are what are called *mercy runs,* search patterns executed to locate lost children, confused elderly people, and campers and hikers who have forgotten or misread their compasses. Clearly it would be counterproductive to have a dog that found a lost child and then ate it. The great bloodhounds are never trained to attack, not by anyone with any respect for their true character.

It is safe to suggest that all of the scent hounds recognized by the American Kennel Club today, all of the scent hounds recognized by the United Kennel Club in Kalamazoo—things like the treeing walker, blue tick, plott, red bone, and others—descended in large part from the bloodhound. There are hounds in Europe not recognized or even seen in this country that also come down to us from the bloodhound in some earlier form, probably around the periphery of the Mediterranean, at least its north and eastern shores, an extremely long time ago.

How do the scent hounds do it? It has been estimated that the bloodhound's nose is two million times as sensitive as the human nose, although I have not the foggiest notion how such calculations can be accurately made. Presumably someone somewhere has done detection tests to determine the lowest parts-per-million-count at which dogs and people can detect the presence of something good or bad. I do not know where or when such tests were done, but everyone goes around repeating that two million number as if it were established fact. By whatever percentage points it might be off, it does convey the essential idea. Scent hounds live on a different plateau than we do when it comes to the sense of smell. We detect a murmur, they enjoy a symphony of odors. We can't even imagine what we are missing, not at that quantum difference.

No one can look at a bloodhound or basset hound or any of the other great sniffers without commenting on their ears. What are known in the trade as *leather*, those marvelous pendulous flaps, have a very important function when it comes to smelling. On the trail the scent hound is seeking particulate matter, bits of dead skin that have scraped off the fleeing felon or wandering youngster. It scrapes away with every movement and floats to the ground. The armpits and crotch are particularly rich mines for this material, which is in fact the scent trail. The areas where the limbs meet the torso create unique smells, apparently, in every human being. So the running person, even the walking person, acts like a bellows spraying the ground with micro-

scopic bits of self. Along comes the dog and those bits forge
into a chain and become a trail. And trails are for running.

On a warm day, air is lighter and tends to rise. The scent
particles rise up with the air, and the dog may charge ahead
with its nose a foot or more off the ground. If it is an
extremely hot day the particles may hang suspended several
feet in the air, and that is when the wise handler rests his
dog in the shade until dusk when things literally settle
down.

If the day is a dank one, however, the scent particles may
tend to cling to the mud and clay, lie low and refuse to move
up to where the dog can sniff them in and expose them to
the computerlike array of nerve endings in its scenting
chamber. Believe it or not, that is where the ears come in.
They hang below the end of the nose, and the dog has only
to move its head back and forth, cast, to have his ear tips
swirl the scent particles up to where he can get a handle on
them. The gender reference "he" at this point is a bit misleading. The best trailers appear to be spayed bitches. They
aren't as likely to be distracted.

How old can a trail be and still be run? According to the
records, the oldest trail successfully tackled by a bloodhound had been laid down 104 hours before. As I said
earlier, the longest trail run was apparently 138 miles. It is
because of these incredible skills that the bloodhound's
findings are treated on a par with human testimony in most
courts in the United States. Two documents are normally
required to qualify the bloodhound as a witness. It must
have AKC papers attesting to the fact that it is a full-
blooded bloodhound and a certificate showing that it was
trained on the trail by an organization like the Police Bloodhound Association. One famous sniffer named Nick Carter

is said to have contributed information in over six hundred criminal cases.

To the bloodhound, the deadly serious business of tracking a rapist-murderer is a lark. What is serious is the trail, and that is a fantastic game, rather like your retriever bounding after a stick as it splashes into the lake or bay. The bloodhound loves the challenge and loves to be praised and rewarded for making a find. All of the sociological complexities of law and order mean nothing to him.

It usually takes little more than an hour or two to get a bloodhound pup interested in the game. With their great loaded-diaper gait they are quickly dragging their handlers all over the lot as people dash and duck, dash and duck. We have owned bloodhounds, among many other breeds, for years, and all that we have owned have loved an opportunity to use their noses. On their rare trips to the city they go fairly wild with the variety and richness of the scent experience. They drop their noses and move out, rarely lifting their heads and frequently walking into parked cars. It is a kind of canine anvil chorus as they thunk from car to car investigating the incredibly lovely scented world of hubcaps. There is so much we humans miss.

A few years back the New York City Police Department decided to run some tests with bloodhounds, using experienced dogs owned by a state police barracks. Two dogs were brought in, although only one was eventually used. The trooper was given a walkie-talkie, as were two detectives sent ahead to lay the trail. The two detectives walked through Central Park side by side. The trooper followed. The police officials were able to coordinate the entire operation from the roof of the Central Park precinct house. I was with them to answer questions and make suggestions.

The high police brass in attendance had already announced that it wouldn't work in an area as crowded as Manhattan, and since high police brass can't be wrong, the test was really quite useless. However, at a predetermined point, the detectives were ordered to split their trail and head off in different directions. One of them dropped his jacket at the point where they split. They were soon out of sight. When the trooper came upon the jacket he went through the brief ritual that signals the dog that he is on duty. The long lead is taken off the choke collar and snapped onto the D-ring on the top of the trailing harness, a custom-made leather rig that has a broad chest plate to absorb the pulling that is inevitable once the trail is detected.

As the lead was switched to the ring, the dog's nose was dropped to the scent article, the sport jacket, and one command given: "Find 'em." The great hound filled his nose with the memory of the jacket and took off at a lope. He had the trail and was for the game.

The dog had his nose on the detective's knee five minutes later as the amazed officer tried to hunker down out of sight in some bushes. He had, after all, been told by the brass that no matter what he witnessed, it wouldn't work. Bloodhounds can't function in big cities. What amazed the detective was the knowledge of the trail he had taken after dropping his jacket. He had cut across an area of Central Park known as the Sheep Meadow. Earlier, there had been a rock concert there and fifty-five thousand people had attended. The detective had cut directly across that unimaginable mass of conflicting scent data. The bloodhound had had no difficulty in keeping on his assigned trail and that one alone. The other fifty-five thousand trails were recognized as extraneous input and ignored.

After the Sheep Meadow the detective had traversed an area where nine softball games were in progress, then cut across an area near the precinct house where people feel safe walking their apartment dogs. Dozens were out there that sunny day. The bloodhound was undeterred by the false input and had his detective in just under five minutes, having never once deviated from the trail.

"Ah, yes," said the somewhat put-out brass, "but they could never handle hydrocarbons!" After these words of bureaucratic wisdom, we instructed the detective to head toward Fifth Avenue, scale the wall out onto the cobblestones, and head north to the roadway that runs across the park and leads as well to the Central Park precinct house. The detective took off, and upon receiving instructions on his radio crossed through a courtyard where two hundred police officers had been mustered for roll call an hour or so earlier. He then headed into and through a repair shop where motorcycles, motorbikes, and police cars were on the racks with their engines running and where the floor was thick with grease and oil. From that veritable salad of hydrocarbons the detective headed into an office building, went into and out of a pistol range, and climbed a flight of stairs to an office. He sat behind the desk and was still panting from his exertions when the bloodhound burst through the door and again laid his great slobbery jaws on his knee waiting to be patted and praised. Having seen all this, the New York City Police brass said, "We told you so," and headed downtown.

One last question about the great slobber-chops, as bloodhounds are affectionately known to many: Why so many wrinkles? The wrinkles testify to loose skin, or the dog's *cape*. Like the long, pendulous ears, the cape has a role to play. A bloodhound on the trail will not stop at brambles and briars or barbed-wire fences. If they lie across the trail they are taken in stride. A tight-skinned dog could hang up, while a loose-skinned dog can always work itself loose with a minimum of damage. The bloodhound's loose skin assures it freedom of movement virtually anywhere it can force its huge frame through. When a bloodhound can't get through, it is its bone structure that hangs it up, not its skin.

That, then, is the ancestry of the scent hounds, the heritage, and the use. Consider now the equally amazing sight of the coursing hounds. The greyhound is certainly an older breed than the bloodhound and couldn't be more different, although both are hounds by definition. Known, as we have said, for at least five thousand years and probably much longer than that, the greyhound is grace itself. It is a dog of the wind, its eyes are the eyes of an eagle, its bone structure an amazing adaptation to grace, speed, and endurance. The deep chest houses huge lungs and a heart to back up the demands that are made on this dog, and its jaws are the slashing instruments of death. A bounding animal must be taken on the fly and snapped to earth and rendered unconscious or dead, all of that in seconds. That is what the greyhound was bred to do and why kings and princes cherished them. It was as if they had captured light, made an adoring slave of a living arrow.

The name "greyhound" is of unknown origin. There are theories. There always are. The ancient Greeks held this breed in high esteem, and *Graius* means "Greek" in Latin. Logically, that *could* have been the source, since the Romans knew the dog from Greece, as they knew so many other cultural enrichments. On the other hand, the British of ancient times thought highly of the breed, and Old English for dog is variously *grech* and *greg*. As logical as the first suggestion, at least. And then there is the fact that greyhounds were predominantly gray in color centuries ago. We will, of course, never be certain, but greyhound it is. The dog is known and admired for its speed, tenacity, and endurance worldwide. In the United States and England the dog is a sporting device as well, and greyhound racing is a common gambling pursuit. Dogs bred especially for the track don't always do well as pets when they retire, and most are destroyed. It is a great shame, but greyhound racing is a harsh business and not at all a game. Interestingly enough, when people are "into" dogs, show dogs and breed them, they are said to be "in the fancy" or "dog fanciers." Again resorting to Old English, *fancy* meant "bet" or "gamble."

What the bloodhound has been to just about all of the scent hounds the greyhound has been to just about all of the fleet sight hounds. Just how much play there was back and forth between the greyhound, the saluki, the afghan, the ibizan hound, the whippet, and all the others and just when it started and stopped can't be established, but there is greyhound blood for certain in all of those breeds, and in the Irish wolfhound and Scottish deerhound as well. And even so distant a working dog as the great dane, although clearly of the mastiff line, may have some greyhound influence way back, perhaps via the Irish wolfhound. During their developmental years, many of the dogs we know today had some intricate and apparently unrecorded breeding done to bring in the nose, eyesight, bone structure, speed, intelligence, coat texture, and endurance of breeds known for these characteristics. Dogs like the greyhound have been around so long and have been so highly regarded as distinct types that it would not be surprising to find their influence cropping up almost anywhere.

I may get my head handed to me for this one, but I am of the opinion that the sight or coursing hounds are not always the smartest dogs on the block. Their skulls do tend to be narrow, and that may properly be seen as indicating reduced brain capacity. Heaven only knows there are exceptions, and I have heard everything but a Ph.D. claimed for this greyhound or that afghan, but the rule is generally acceptable, I think, that you can't teach a sight hound relativity.

That can spell problems when one of these incredible lightning bolts gets loose. Obedience, a good quick response to *come* or *sit* or *stay*, may not work too well. Given the amount of ground a coursing hound can cause to pass beneath it in a matter of seconds, a beast on the loose may mean one lost forever. I have seen afghans get loose at dog shows and clear fences and vanish, some never to be seen again. In Manhattan I saw a magnificent apricot-colored afghan with a perfect coat loose and running. It was dragging a leash. There was no apparent owner in pursuit. He or she had probably been left fifty blocks behind seconds before. I pulled my car up to a fireplug and took off after the dog, along with several other people, some of them dragging their own dogs along by the lead. It was soon a posse, but we might as well have been chasing a northeast gale. No one could get near the animal, and it was becoming more panic-stricken by the second. It was so soon out of sight that we didn't have a chance to get winded. Heaven alone knows what happened to it. People with coursing hounds in the city should hang on to the leash. Up over the wrist and across the palm of the hand, with fingers clenched, that is the rule. It is that or, sooner or later, no dog.

The greyhound is an enormously interesting animal not just because of its history, but because of its nature. There

is a lighter, faster variety with more powerful hindquarters
bred for the track and others are bred for pets. The pet dog
is so fast it doesn't seem possible that track dogs could be
faster yet, but they are. The greyhound is a high stepper, it
has a dignity and a grace, and every footprint it makes seems
like a work of art. They tend to look a bit fragile because
they are so meatless, but what is there is steel wire and
perfect coordination. Dogs off the track need not die. They
can be turned around, although they could be tricky with
cats and shouldn't be given access to rabbits and other small
native game. They have been trained to go for it; that is
what makes them run.

Owners of coursing hounds know things about their dogs
that no one can know until they have joined the ranks of the
converted. That is true of all dogs, however; they belong to
humankind in the grand overview, but to a select group of
people in a very special way. Ask someone who has raised
a litter of afghan puppies, who has tied the cords, sat up all
night, helped the bitch by tube-feeding the babies. Ask
them and see if you come even close to knowing that breed.
Breed fanciers are an elite, and do they ever know it!

About a hundred years ago in England, or perhaps just
a little longer ago than that, it was decided it would be nice
to have a greyhound in miniature, although one still able to
play the gaming animal. The whippet was developed to
chase rabbits around an enclosure, a somewhat milder sport
than bull and bear baiting with bulldogs and mastiff breeds.
The whippet is used as a racing animal to this day, although
it is more often seen as a pet than its ancestor the greyhound is. The whippet is the epitome of grace and is simply
incapable of assuming an undignified or clumsy attitude. It
looks like porcelain and acts like a tern on the wing. It loves
its family, and to take one out for a run is an athletic experi-

ence few other pastimes can equal. Except for their intoler-
ance of cold, whippets are far hardier than they look. They
are also somewhat brighter.

Perhaps because they have been used more as pets and
less for field work than the other true coursing hounds,
whippets are virtually perfect house animals. They do need
to run, though, and they absolutely insist on an enormous
amount of attention. They can be obedience-trained, and
for people who like the concept of a piece of sculpture that
can be signaled to life and trusted to outrun its own shadow,
the whippet is the dog. The relatively few that are still used
on the track are seldom encountered in the pet end of
things, but they are generally redeemable and there is no
need to destroy them when their winning days are over,
often when they are still very young. The whippet, like its
forebear the ancient greyhound, is history and grace, style
and tradition, love in a skinny dog.

About two thousand years ago, as far as we can tell, the
Italians got the idea of shrinking their noble greyhound into
a pocket version that would be called upon to work at only
one task, making people happy. The Italian greyhound
evolved, a weakened but nonetheless lovely version of its
larger ancestor, the killer of the field. Today we do not
recognize the Italian greyhound as a hound but show it as
a toy.

On the walls of Pompeii there can be found the inscrip-
tion *cave canem,* "beware of dog." For years it was assumed
that warning referred to the mastiff-type guard dogs
wealthy families kept chained near their doors or loose in
their courtyards to discourage bandits and other elements
in the local crime wave. (We did not invent crime in modern
times. It has always played a major role in the development
of dog types.) It is thought now, however, that the admoni-

tion common in Pompeii did not refer to guard dogs at all but rather to the diminutive Italian greyhounds that were the mark of wealth and position in a Roman city of the time. The idea was not to worry about being bitten by a dog, but rather not to step on the dog or slam the gate on him.

Whatever may have been the case in Pompeii of ill fortune, the Italian greyhound became the absolute darling of European royalty and sat beside many a throne and on a great many laps few other creatures ever got to see close up, much less sit on. By the time the breed reached England, early in the 1600s, Charles I was in power and the breed was already the signature of the privileged, by virtue of their wealth, blood, or position. The dog became favored in the British Isles by the few who could afford an example. As might be expected of a dog whose paw print was like the royal hand of the king himself, there are legends. Perhaps it is true that Lobengula, the last of the great Kafir kings in South Africa, did adorn his 350-pound person with an Italian greyhound for which he had paid two hundred head of cattle. Perhaps Frederick the Great, king of Prussia, did carry his Italian greyhound with him wherever he went on the saddle before him, and perhaps he did kneel weeping in his garden burying his favorite with his bare hands under a rose bush. There are more than a few such stories about the hound that got shrunken right out of its group.

The Working Group represent eighteen breeds recognized in the United States. Working Group entries *today* are:

Akita   Bernese Mountain Dog
Alaskan Malamute   Boxer

Bullmastiff   Mastiff
Doberman Pinscher   Newfoundland
Giant Schnauzer   Rottweiler
Great Dane   St. Bernard
Great Pyrenees   Samoyed
Komondor   Siberian Husky
Kuvasz   Standard Schnauzer

There are obviously misleading names on the list. The great dane has had nothing to do with Denmark nor Denmark with it. The name as we know it apparently came into the English from French, where the mastiff descendant, specialist in boar hunting, was called the *grand danois* or "big Danish." (It is unlikely that they were referring to pastry.) The French also called the breed the German mastiff or *dogue allemand*. Several hundred years ago the word *mastiff* in English, *dogge* in German and related languages, and *dogue* and *dogo* in Latin and Romance languages all were roughly equivalent, referring to large-boned dogs with massive heads. Anyway, we still call this dog of clearly German origin the great dane, much to the amazement of the Germans and the amusement of the Danes.

"Giant schnauzer" and "standard schnauzer" are again names that confuse the unwary and confound the forgetful. The schnauzer lines—please note the plural—probably evolved in Württemberg and Bavaria. There are actually three recognized in this country; the miniature schnauzer, unlike its working-dog namesake, is shown in the Terrier Group. The standard schnauzer is the oldest of the three, but what is most important is that all three evolved separately, from different original stock almost certainly, and have converged with relatively little interbreeding, none of it in recent times. It is a remarkable case, and it can be confusing to hear the terms "miniature," "standard," and "giant" applied to schnauzer. That would seem to imply one dog in three sizes, instead of three different dogs. The latter is the case.

All three schnauzers make excellent watchdogs, although their lineage is so very different. The giant is most impressive; it is so large that fanciers of the breed use it to pull carts. The schnauzer of smallest size, the miniature, is, like all of the terriers with which it is grouped, noisy when intruders appear. It doesn't have the basso profundo of the larger dogs, but it can put up enough thunder to advise intruders that they are no longer unnoticed. Being unnoticed is what skulkers in the night want, and any good noisy dog can rob them of that. All schnauzers are good at the task.

The schnauzer face is one of the most enchanting in all dogdom. Whiskers *en bush* do something for a dog, and so do bushy eyebrows. The little salt-and-pepper to black miniatures are enormously popular, and when well groomed—not a task every private owner does as well as it might be done—they are enchanting. One thing, though—the miniature schnauzer will not be denied its time for interaction. They demand patting, usually get all they want, and then demand more minutes later. They also expect to have rubber toys tossed and tossed again. That is their divine right. It is, in fact, just about impossible to convince a miniature schnauzer that it is not itself divine. They are terribly self-centered, but extraordinary companions. Their range is universal, insofar as human playmates go. The very elderly find their liveliness, their love affair with life, intriguing. Kids find them ideal participants in all manner of games. They appeal to everyone and walk with a step that proves that they know it. You don't have to tell a miniature schnauzer that it is a good boy or good girl. They darn well already know it themselves. What it comes down to in their minds, I am sure, is whether you are good enough for them.

Schnauzers, and particularly the miniature schnauzer, are like poodles a breed that people get very silly about. You are far more likely to find the poodle or the miniature schnauzer wearing a diamond-studded collar than any other breed. People often comment on that adversely, usually in relationship or at least with reference to starving children in Biafra. Diamond-studded collars and mink coats, of course, have nothing at all to do with dogs or dog-owning. The name of the game is ostentation, and there is little difference between gussying up a dog with diamonds and wearing solid-gold Coors Beer belt buckles or million-dollar diamond rings yourself. People who can afford extreme luxury frequently indulge in it, and if they elect to mix diamonds and dogs there is little the dog can do about it, since it can't even recognize what is going on. Buying your schnauzer, or any other dog, thirty-seven custom hand-knit sweaters from an extremely expensive store, as one New Yorker has been reported to do, is again playing games with being rich. It has nothing to do with dogs. Nothing of that kind does. Ah, but how often dogs take the rap.

The Working Group has dogs of enormously varying antiquity and with histories that range from the carefully detailed to the wholly unknown. The magnificent great Pyrenees or *le grand chien des montagnes* (also, in England, the Pyrean mountain dog) dates back about four thousand years to the Bronze Age in Europe. Much earlier than that, it is believed, it was found in Central Asia and perhaps even as far to the east as Siberia. All confusing, largely conjecture, but clearly the legends surround a breed of enormous antiquity whose travels are bewildering. About all we can say about that for sure is that they couldn't have done it on their own. They were transported. Again, we can with good reason guess that there was once an important traffic in certain breeds of dogs as items of commerce.

There is another working dog that was evolved for roughly the same kind of work, as a guard dog. It is the doberman pinscher, and it is a breed so young and so well documented that we even know who did the work. His name, not at all surprisingly, was Louis Dobermann, and he lived in Apolda, in Thueringen, Germany. He did his work in the 1890s, and he used traditional German-shepherd stock of uncertain origin and added rottweiler, terrier, and a smooth-coated dog we call the German pinscher. He got his dog, and we still have it. It is now the second most popular dog in the United States by AKC registrations. It is exceeded in esteem only by the three poodles combined under one heading. If the poodles were listed separately, as are, for example, the schnauzers, the doberman pinscher, one of the youngest breeds known to dogdom, would rank as king of the full-bred dogs of America. It is admired worldwide as a superb athlete, a splendid, loyal guard with extraordinary good looks. Its chiseled refinement makes it appear to me to be the Luger pistol of the dog world. It looks dangerous. It also looks as if it could do anything it was asked to do, and it usually can. The original hot temperament of the breed that gave it a well-deserved reputation for trickiness has mellowed to the point where it is now used to lead the blind. It is not always the most trustworthy dog around strange animals, but it is loyal to master, hearth, and home. Its rise in popularity during recent years, due in no small part, I am sure, to the fear of crime, has been meteoric. One expects Louis Dobermann to have a statue erected to him at any moment.

As a child growing up in Massachusetts and as a young man in California and later New York, I had a not terribly well-veiled sense of foreboding when I had to handle a doberman. In two veterinary hospitals in which I worked, kennel help were not expected to lift dobies onto the examining table for the veterinarian; their owners were. One veterinarian I worked for wouldn't touch a doberman until it had been muzzled.

In New York, many years ago, I lived next door to a man who owned a doberman that was notorious throughout the neighborhood. It had killed several cats and at least two dogs. Warnings from police and judges had no effect. The man would not keep his dog leashed. He would step out of his apartment house with his doberman by his side, and if another animal happened to be in sight the doberman was off like a bolt from a crossbow.

There is not a doberman alive incapable of such attacks, but dobermans generally aren't like that now. What the doberman fanciers have accomplished is nothing less than miraculous. A few months ago we had house guests for the weekend and they brought a young doberman bitch with them. She fit into a house full of strange people, cats, and dogs and never once offered a problem. She made an instant adjustment.

I sincerely hope that the doberman's public-relations person can keep pace with the breeders' accomplishments. The doberman that people of my generation were raised to fear, even those of us who clearly were destined to have animal-related careers, is to be found only rarely today. The doberman pinscher, once the cocked pistol of dogdom, is now more often a magnificently sleek and athletic pussycat. I wouldn't want to try coming in off a fire escape and encounter one in the middle of the night (they are territorial), but in any reasonable situation a doberman that has been well socialized and obedience-trained is a fine pet. There is, in my estimation, no better looking dog. For anyone seeking a macho image or wanting to walk down the street un-mugged, the doberman has it all going for it. Did you ever hear of anyone walking a doberman pinscher being mo-lested? I never did. At times, a hateful reputation has much to recommend it.

The Working Group is fairly unusual in that it has no dogs assigned to it that could not work in an original way if called upon to do so. The dachshunds among the hounds could no longer go to ground after a badger, and most cocker spaniels (American version) can no longer be effec-tive in the field unless drastically altered by being put into genetic reverse. But the Working Group appears to contain dogs that all have at least the physical ability to do what they were designed to do, however long ago that design left the drawing board.

There is another consideration when evaluating the Working Group as a logical grouping: a good many dogs were designed as multipurpose animals, just as they were in the Sporting Group. The akita, for example, was a guard dog and a hunter in Japan. These are the breeds that helped mankind survive over thousands of years and under ever-changing conditions. They are adaptable, most of them, and have more than earned their keep.

I am generally not a mystic, but I do find an endearing quality of mystery in the northern spitz breeds, some but not all of which have been siphoned off to other groups, the Norwegian elkhound to the Hound Group and the kees-hond to the Nonsporting Group. The Siberian husky, the samoyed, the Alaskan malamute, and the akita are all work-ing dogs still. (The toy pomeranian was certainly of this lineage, too, but has been shrunk drastically. It is a fraction of its original size.)

There is something about these northern sled dogs, possibly the wolf in them. The samoyed from Siberia (same general turf as the husky) is undoubtedly one of the purest dog breeds we know today, but I am sure the stories of Eskimos still allowing wolf blood into husky and malamute lines are true.

A few days before this was written I witnessed a scene with a husky that I will never understand. Nor, I doubt, will anyone else. The Humane Society of the United States is a modern steel-and-glass office building in downtown Washington, D.C., at 21st and L Streets NW. It is a perfectly fine-looking building, but if you were rushing along on either 21st Street or L Street you would not pay it any special attention. It looks rather like the other banks and society buildings that surround it. No animals are kept there, of course. It is a policy and planning center, not an animal shelter.

The other day when I was there it had just snowed. Out front the tracks told the story. A lone dog of considerable size, unaccompanied by a human being, had walked down 21st Street, passing, obviously, scores of other buildings, and had turned very deliberately up the walk to the front door of the HSUS building. There it sat and waited for the first office workers to arrive. By the time I got there the record in tracks was still out front, and I was taken out to examine them. The Siberian husky was happily settled into an office on the second floor. He had no collar and was quite content to wait it out until someone there broke down and took him home. They had already sent out for food for him.

How in the name of dogdom did this one dog pick this one office building out of thousands in downtown Washington in the middle of a snowstorm? There was no barking from within, no smell of other animals, just a sign that announced the purpose of the structure. I insist on believing the husky couldn't read the sign. How else, then? Coincidence? O.K., but that is the coward's way out.

There is something spooky about the sled dogs, and I mean that in a nice way. Our old husky, Oomiac, who only recently went to the great ice field in the sky, would vanish, simply dissolve, and then reappear whining and posturing for affection. I have raced with a samoyed across a frozen beach on the rocky coasts of wintry Maine and seen that magnificent white giant stand on a promontory looking out to sea. It knew something I did not know, although I don't know what it was or even what it was about. I just sensed it. You could call and for a minute or two it wouldn't hear you. It wasn't disobedience, it was simply disconnected from this world. Then it would turn and come galumphing through the snow ready for the game, any game. It had returned from someplace. I often wondered where it was. What do these dogs hear? What summons them? They are warm and affectionate animals, they have rich internal lives, and when they externalize and when they keep it all in to themselves is up to them. Or is it? Is there something from some other place that signals to them for connection and disconnection? I wonder often and learn nothing.

I have referred often to the mastiff line, and indeed it has been, like those of the greyhound and the bloodhound, one of the foundation lines for today's incredible roster of great dog breeds. In the last century it was used yet another time to produce one of the most delightful of all the giants, the bullmastiff.

The problem was on private estates, and it came at night. Gamekeepers on the prowl for poachers were prowled at

right back and often beaten or even killed by people who
were becoming restive about British class distinction and
privilege. Something had to be done, and the ancient mastiff of (probably) Tibet and Mongolia and later Rome was
called upon. When allowed to be aggressive or taught to
attack, a pure mastiff could be rather more than was needed.
It was therefore crossed with another breed with a leather-
tough heritage, the bulldog.

Not at all surprisingly, the result of the bulldog-mastiff
cross produced a dog of enormous power. It was first called
the gamekeeper's night dog and later that was changed to
bullmastiff. It was quickly recognized as a separate breed. In
those days of night patrol the dog was preferred in the
darkest colors possible, black being very much preferred.
That made it, of course, more difficult to see. That is not the
case today. The bullmastiff was bred and trained to attack
in a unique way. It wasn't supposed to bite, not really, just
keep the gamekeeper's adversary off his feet. The bullmastiff hits hard, and if the foe tries to stand the dog hits again.
It is an inexorable force. When absolutely necessary—if, for
instance, the man is armed—the bullmastiff will take a forearm between its massive jaws and apply pressure, steadily,
until the bone is about to break and the handler tells his dog
to cool it. This is a tough, tough breed.

Friends in the next village own a pair of bullmastiffs, and
one of them recently came through a second-floor screen
and hit the ground far below at a full run. A strange dog was
on the lawn. On another occasion a gardener was giving my
friend a bad time. He had, I believe, been drinking, and he
made the mistake of raising both his voice and his arm. A
bullmastiff took the front door off its hinges and the man
was flat on his back with a really menacing bullmastiff face
only inches from his own. The growl came from deep inside

the breed's history. When the man tried to struggle with the dog—a very silly thing to do—the old forearm trick was brought into play. The man cried uncle very quickly and was shown off the property.

An evening with our friends is a joy. As you stand with your cocktail in hand you are usually taken behind the knees by a dog about the size and build of a Sherman tank. No one ever pats a bullmastiff; you thump and pound them. You couldn't hurt one. They are true bulls and among the most pleasant dogs I know. Just, please, don't make threatening sounds or gestures at their owners. As watchdogs and companions for children they are without serious challenge. Heaven help anyone who tried to harm the child of the family.

The rottweiler is rather like the mastiff and the bullmastiff in that it has a massive head, staggeringly powerful jaws, and a sense of duty when it comes to hearth and family. They are all of that same ancient protection-dog lineage.

In Germany, as the rottweiler evolved from Roman mastiffs brought by invading legions, it was used as a drover as well as a guard. The breed became particularly good at managing cattle, and then farmers found an even more specialized use. Once a cattleman and his droving rottweilers had gotten the cattle to market and the cash had changed hands, there was that trek home. Highwaymen and bandits with less romantic names were frequently encountered. A man could lose much of a year's income in a matter of moments, if not his life. Ah, but there were the dogs.

Farmers returning from market simply put their newly acquired cash in a leather pouch and attached it to the collar of one of their dogs. That usually did it. They got home with their money intact.

Rottweilers today may not be called upon to play Brinks

and transport the family fortune, but there is no doubt that a burglar checking out your home is likely to go elsewhere if a rottweiler is on the premises. This is one of the steadiest, most reliable of all breeds, one of the best family protectors there is, but it is a pet first and foremost. I have known not just a few rottweilers but have never known anyone to have a bad time with one that had had even basic obedience training. They get on well with other animals that have a modicum of respect for their rights. They do not, however, suffer fools gladly. Other dogs should not snarl at them. They do, after all, carry the blood of dogs that drove off wolves, bears, and bandits in the mountains of Tibet; they were bred and trained in Germany to keep highwaymen at bay—who would want to growl at such a dog?

5

Diversity II: The Terriers, Toys, Nonsporting Dogs, and Herding Dogs

The stunning ability of the dog to change its form on command, its size, shape, and color, and our need to order up these changes has cemented our two species together in what appears to be an eternal friendship. Our most popular companion animal just *had* to be a quick-change artist, and our good old accommodating friend had become just that. That level of elasticity is seen in a few domestic plants—cabbage, cauliflower, brussels sprouts, and kale are all one species—but nowhere else among domestic animals. Our unique friendship exists because the dog's ability to accommodate itself to our tastes is unique.

It should be stressed that the dog, strictly speaking, was not *domesticated,* although it is now certainly domestic. The dog has no truly wild counterpart; it is the descendant of a species that was sufficiently capable of socialization so that

man could begin genetic engineering, based on what knowledge heaven alone knows. That is a big part of the cynological mystery. The wolf was socialized, and the dog that has
evolved from it is a wholly new species. Again, being as
accommodating as we could hope for, the dog brought the
best of wolf characteristics along with it, things like pack
behavior and the potential for good manners.

The meaning of the word "species" is best not dealt with
at length here, because it is *supposed* to refer to discreet,
self-contained kinds of plants and animals that breed only
with their own kind. Dogs and wolves still breed readily, and
all of their offspring are by no means "mules" or nonrepro-
ducing. If we had to adhere to some strict doctrine regard-
ing the word "species" there might be a perfectly valid
argument for not assigning the dog its own species at all,
but leaving it as a subspecies under *Canis lupus familiaris.*
However, the people who know all about these things have
in their wisdom assigned the dog its own species designation, *Canis familiaris,* and we should go along with that and
wonder only at the incredible flexibility of this man-made
creature. Consider, as we shall in this chapter, the chihuahua, the bulldog, and the standard poodle. Quite a spread.

On to the groups. Group Number Four is the Terrier
Group. There are twenty-three terrier breeds recognized by
the American Kennel Club, and all but three originated
entirely in the British Isles. The terriers known today are:

Airedale	Cairn
American Staffordshire	Dandie Dinmont
Australian	Fox
Bedlington	Irish
Border Bull	Kerry Blue
Bull	Lakeland

Manchester	Sealyham
Miniature Schnauzer	Skye
Norfolk	Soft-Coated Wheaten
Norwich	Staffordshire Bull
Scottish	Welsh

West Highland White

Before getting into the Terrier Group in detail it should be noted that there is no breed recognized as the pit bull terrier, a breed that everyone seems to know everything about except the fact that it doesn't exist according to the American Kennel Club. The United Kennel Club does register a breed called the APBT, the American pit bull terrier.

Please also note that the Yorkshire terrier and the Tibetan terrier are not terriers either. They are in the Nonsporting Group, the next to last group of recognized breeds to be discussed. But now, the Terrier Group.

Once upon a time, all small, relatively compact dogs that weren't clearly something else were called terriers or "earth dogs," from *terra,* Latin for "earth." That name arose because the terriers went to earth, dug into tunnels, and plunged down holes after their prey. Large dogs were called mastiffs and hunting dogs were called spaniels or setters. Those names in themselves, therefore, aren't terribly revealing, especially when we encounter them in older literature. They did not necessarily mean then what they mean now.

Terriers are generally but not always smallish dogs with a fire inside that simply cannot be quenched. They are scrappy, playful, sometimes hyperactive, generally exceedingly loyal characters. They are the clowns of the dog world and are expected, even in the show ring, to be hard on each other. As for other animals, everything is for chasing. I remember watching the lakeland terriers being judged at the Westminster Kennel Club Dog Show a few years ago in Madison Square Garden. I announce that show in the evening and generally film it for television during the day. Any time I can get to myself to wander around and just enjoy the dogs is special time. I was watching the lakelands being judged with enormous pleasure when a mouse suddenly appeared. Who knows whether it dropped from the rafters and somehow survived that terrible fall, or whether it ran out from under the stands, or whether someone with a perverse sense of humor turned it loose? At any rate, there it was, a mouse at a dog show. Spectators, stewards, handlers, and the judge were all taken by surprise, but that was nothing compared to the reaction of the dogs. Never in the history of the lakeland terrier breed or in the history of dog shows has there been a better bunch of lakelands on view. Forgotten were the endless rounds of the ring; forgotten, too, were the proddings of the handlers and judges and the hours of grooming that went before. All there was was the mouse and each individual dog, and each individual dog looked as sharp as it possibly could.

Of course, all of the dogs were on leads. One can only imagine with a mixture of mild horror and considerable amusement what would have happened if those born rat-catchers had been loose. What a pile of very expensive fur that would have been! As it was, all they could do was set themselves up smartly, a whole string of square little red dogs with arched necks, tails pointing toward the dome, noses down and eyes flashing fire. It was like a doggy fire drill. They remained on full alert long after the mouse had vanished. The intruder's progress across the arena floor was not difficult to follow, stringing behind it, as it did, a series of human yelps and squeals, doggy barks and blasts, and people popping up out of folding wooden chairs as if they were spring-laden. The lakelands were at their best, inspired by the intrusive mouse, while a great many people were at their silly worst. The ultimate fate of the Westminster Mouse was never revealed, but he certainly had his moment of glory. He got Best-in-Rodent for that day.

Intruders in dog shows at Madison Square Garden are not really all that unusual. In 1982, at the 106th running of the show (it is the second-oldest continuous sporting event in America, beaten only by the Kentucky Derby and that by only one year), two cats kept popping out from under the stands and chasing each other around the periphery of the group judging area. They appeared again and again and had the dogs, who were supposed to be on their very best behavior, fairly bursting with anxiety. Periodically, individuals and delegations would present themselves to Chief Steward Robert Taylor and announce the intruder. "Did you know . . . ?" "Did you see . . . ?" Of course, Bob *did* and *had.* The Westminster Kennel Club Dog Show is a terrific strain on the show committee, who work twenty-hour days for at least four days to see that all goes off well at America's most prestigious canine happening. When you are very, very tired and are told the same thing over and over again to the point of near nausea, tempers can shorten considerably. Complainer after complainer was sent packing with what became Bob's stock answer. "We don't intend to do anything about it unless one of them wins something." Prickliness, particularly at an exhausting dog show, is admirable. It also does an important task in preserving sanity where the edge is very fine.

The king of the terriers is without a doubt the splendid

airedale. This twenty-three-inch tall dog is surely descended from an extinct English dog we know now as the black-and-tan. No one knows where the black-and-tan came from or, indeed, the terrier line itself. It is believed that the airedale and the Irish, fox, and Welsh terriers at least arose from that old breed and perhaps most of the other terriers from them. Apparently the original black-and-tan varied tremendously in size, from fifteen to over thirty pounds. That was typical of dogs once upon a time. The emphasis was on utility, not conformation. Life in rawer times was less often a beauty contest. Different breeders had different uses for their gaming dogs—the pursuit of badger, fox, weasel, rats (particularly water rats), otter, anything that would run and give sport. The dogs were agile and seemingly incapable of tiring, with good eyesight and keen hearing. Then as now, courage was an expected ingredient of any animal worthy of being called terrier. Otterhounds were in use in the English river valleys, and there was some breeding back and forth between the otterhound and the black-and-tan, perhaps to make the otterhound less phlegmatic and to give the terriers a sharper nose and increased power in the water. How much went in which direction can no longer be ascertained, but there is terrier in the otterhound, and some terriers have very good noses. The black-and-tan has apparently come down to us in a very much more refined form as the Manchester terrier, or so many British dog authorities suggest.

Slowly the terrier types began to emerge. There were working terriers (that was an actual breed), waterside terriers, and Bingley terriers. Refinement continued, and by 1879, at an agricultural show in the town of Bingley in Yorkshire, there was a class for airedale terriers. The show was staged by the Airedale Agricultural Society. By 1883 the Welsh terrier was recognized as a distinct type. The smooth fox terrier had been ahead of them, because by 1862 he had been recognized in a show at Birmingham. But the airedale was off and running. Shortly after 1879 the Bingley example was followed in the towns of Skipton, Bradford, Keighley, and Otley. The biggest win an airedale could achieve in those days was a gold medal at Otley.

One airedale dog is generally considered to be the trunk from which the tree grew. He was Champion Master Briar, and he lived to be nine years old, from 1897 to 1906. One of his sons, Champion Clonmel Monarch, was sent out to Philadelphia, and that dog became the foundation animal of the airedale in America. A dog was born in 1919 in the United States who was named Warland Ditto. He went on to become the king of the breed in America. He lived for eight years, dying in 1927. It is highly likely that any good airedale today will trace back to him. His descendants are now found all over the world. It is not unusual to find, in any species of domestic animal or in any breed of dog, a single specimen upon which history was built. It is generally known during that animal's lifetime that that is to be the case. Think of the joy of that: eternal celebrity, an animal for all time asking to be taken for a walk.

In Elizabethan England there was a form of stocky, low-built, bull-necked fighting dog of enormous power, stamina, and courage that provided sport for cruel people in very cruel times. This was a bulldog, although it was probably called many other things besides that. The dog fought anything that was thrown to it. Bulldogs were fighting bulls or at least baiting them in every marketplace in the country. Manchester terriers or black-and-tans, perhaps, were fighting rats in pits, as were any number of other terrier types. People were betting on animal combat just as they had in ancient Rome. Animals died by the tens of thousands, and that included the dogs themselves as well as the bait animals. Bears were imported from Europe and North America and chained to trees for dogs to worry. People watched in fascination as the animals screamed and the blood flowed. It was a terrible misuse of the victimized animals and of the dogs employed in the games. As always, the dogs were the extensions of their owners. Brutal people created brutal dogs.

There were, of course, people of more refined sensitivities, and they objected and eventually they won. Virtually all of those sports are now outlawed in most civilized lands.

The dogs used in these combats varied according to the size of the animals they were expected to kill or at least mangle. Terrier blood was prominent, and so was bulldog blood (please note, when we come to the Nonsporting Group, the proper name of that breed is simply bulldog, not *English* bull as is so often heard). Bull and terrier crosses undoubtedly gave rise to the bull terrier back in the 1830s. The terrier used was probably a breed we generally refer to today as the white English terrier, a breed that has apparently become extinct. The impetus to breed ever better sporting dogs encouraged extinction. As soon as a breeder had a better terrier, one that could win more money in the games or more praise in the field, the older breeds were simply dropped. It does not take a breed of dog long to become extinct, usually not more than fifteen years.

Initially that cross was known as the bull *and* terrier, not the bull terrier. It is believed that the Spanish pointer was used, and in the 1860s a breeder named James Hinks was able to breed all-white versions of the breed, and to this day the bull terrier is recognized for registration purposes in two varieties, the colored and the white, although they are precisely the same dog. The wisdom of this practice is somewhat questionable, as shown at a recent running of the Westminster. Litter mates won Best-of-Variety, and there were two animals, brother and sister, competing under different banners in the same ring—bull terrier colored variety and bull terrier white variety. The same thing could happen with the cocker spaniel, too, of course. You could conceivably have three animals in the ring from the same litter—a black cocker, a particolor cocker, and an ASCOB (Any Solid Color Other than Black). Why color variation should be recognized in a few breeds and not in all others is not clear. After all, Newfoundlands come in black and brown, bronze and landseer (black and white). Salukis come in white, cream, fawn, golden, red grizzle, and tan tricolor as well as black and tan. The vagaries of purebred dog recognition and definition will seemingly never end. Recognizing two or three color varieties in two breeds while ignoring it in others would seem to open one enormously large can of worms.

There were, of course, romanticized views of fighting dogs and equally romantic names. The bull terrier was called the "gladiator" and the white version, which became very fashionable, rather like wearing Gucci shoes, was called "the white cavalier." We have two other former combat terrier breeds recognized by the American Kennel Club today. The Staffordshire bull terrier emerged from those nineteenth-century crosses of terrier and bulldog. Probably what was known as the bulldog terrier became the Staffordshire bull terrier. The old pit bull terrier that dated back to Elizabethan times when bull and bear baiting were popular was almost certainly what Mr. Hinks used initially to develop his all-white bull terrier.

The anticruelty movement in England picked up so much support in the 1800s that the Staffordshire bull terrier was refused recognition by the kennel club there. With royal patronage, the Royal Society for the Prevention of Cruelty to Animals was unalterably opposed to giving any support to breeders of fighting dogs. Although the bull terrier was recognized, the Staffordshire bull terrier was scorned. Finally, in 1935, the ban was lifted and the Staffordshire bull terrier (I keep repeating the full name for a reason that will become clear in a moment) was recognized not as a fighting dog, but as a former fighting dog suitable for human companionship. In March 1975 that breed was finally shown under its rightful name in America as well. It had been a long process, but man cannot create civilized dogs until he himself is a reasonably civilized being. Our dogs are only what we need or at least want them to be.

Ah, but there is yet another change. In 1935 the American Kennel Club recognized the Staffordshire terrier as distinct from the Staffordshire bull terrier, but that name was changed again, to American Staffordshire terrier, in 1972. So what we have today is the bull terrier (white and colored varieties), the American Staffordshire terrier (nineteen inches tall and preferably less than 80 percent white and not all white), and the Staffordshire bull terrier (up to sixteen inches tall and any of a number of colors sometimes mixed with white). And, of course, there is the American pit bull terrier listed by the United Kennel Club. All of these breeds have an undeserved reputation, because most people, first, confuse the breeds and, second, know just enough English history to have a deep-seated prejudice against them. They are almost universally thought of as "vicious." Like so much "common knowledge" on any subject, that is nonsense. The word "vicious" is not properly applied to dogs anyway. People can be vicious. Dogs may at times reflect that fact.

Former fighting-terrier breeds are generally bred as pets in America today. Like all terriers they can be but are not necessarily tricky with other animals, dogs included. They are fine companions, good friends, and as trustworthy as any other fiery terrier breed. They should be trained, but then all dogs should be. They are loving and loyal, and I can't imagine what else a dog is supposed to be. Their marvelous musculature, their nice solid "thumpy" feeling, is terribly appealing. Their incredible self-confidence is downright inspiring.

But there are still dogfights in America. There are still people who cannot get the caveman out of their system, who still raise dogs to tear each other apart. The practice is against the law in almost every state, but it is so open that magazines are published to announce breedings, meets, and records. *Pit Dogs* and *Sporting Dog Journal* are two of them. They are distributed through the United States mail although they advertise, record, foster, and abet a wholly illegal activity. The post office has all kinds of rules about what can be mailed and what cannot be mailed, but it has consistently turned away from control of this horror. The excuse usually given by the post office is that it doesn't make the rules, Congress does. That is bureaucratic nonsense, because the post office traditionally asks Congress for rules and Congress gives the agency what it wants. There is, somewhere, a lobby strong enough to keep the United States Postal Service looking the other way while dogs tear each other apart and rednecks shriek and howl and place

very, very large bets. It is said that hundreds of thousands
of dollars may change hands at large meets, and there is
more than a little suggestion that organized crime is behind
the growing underground attraction. Young dogs destined
for the ring are given kittens to practice on. Traditionally,
cats and sometimes small dogs are suspended overhead and
the pit dogs are encouraged to leap up and tear them apart.

The dogs used? Staffordshire blood, predominantly, and
American pit bull terrier, judging from the dogs' appearance, but it goes back to the bulldog-terrier mix, all the way
back to bull and bear baiting in the sixteenth and seventeenth centuries and pit-dog fighting in the nineteenth century. It all really goes back to the brute in all of us.

It seems to me two things matter in the situation today.
First, the underground pit-dog circuit should be wiped out
and four fine breeds of terriers should not be marked by
something over which they have no control. They may have
common ancestry with the fighting dogs of today, but they
are not a part of the same scene. As for the people who
engage in dogfighting in modern times, they have little
minds and no souls. By definition we can reasonably expect
that their counterparts will always be with us. It is a pity that
they have to use anything as venerable as the dog for their
kicks. Why can't they just do it to each other?

When I was a boy growing up in Methuen, Massachusetts
(or at least trying to), there was a man down the street who
had a bull terrier named Mackerel. The unusual name, I
believe, came from his shiny coat and some rather peculiar
brindle marks along his sides. Mack, as we called him, was
kept in a fenced yard, and everyone just assumed that he
was a positive terror. We were led to believe, as most people
were, that his was a killer breed on a par with the much-
maligned doberman pinscher. Poor Mack watched kids

stream by on the other side of the fence going to and from school, but nobody would stop to talk to him. We had been warned. There was even a padlock on his gate. Mack had long since given up barking at the kids going by. He just looked dejected and lonely. When he was taken out for a walk it was on a heavy chain lead, and if you encountered his burly owner with dog on a public thoroughfare you crossed the street.

One morning the yard was empty, the padlock was missing; Mack was gone. At just about the same time a Boston terrier that lived down the street, the passionately beloved pet of a terrible old lady who had to be twice as mean as Mack, no matter how mean he was supposed to be, vanished, too. That Boston played in its backyard without a fence. Clearly Mack had killed it. The scenario was clear to see. Some psychopath had opened Mack's gate, and when he had been turned out from his normally secure yard he, ever the killer, had gone on the hunt.

The police were called immediately. We were told by our parents that they had orders to shoot Mack on sight. There would be no trial. Guilt was assumed.

Things got very much worse two days later when another pet in the neighborhood vanished without a trace. It was a cross, as I recall, of a cocker spaniel and something fairly indistinct. Mack the killer dog was obviously still in the area, still killing, and the hunt intensified. Some people put loaded guns near their windows and doors. Kids were walked to and from approved play areas, particularly the smaller kids. Who knew where Mack would stop?

Then, about five days after he had vanished, Mack reappeared with his two friends, the Boston and the cocker-whatever mix in tow, in a playground. A woman who immediately went into something like total hysteria encountered a bunch of kids surrounding the three dogs, patting and hugging them. Mack was nearly wiggling his tail end off with joy. He loved kids and had been so benignly persuasive a leader of his own kind that he had been able to lure the other two dogs out of their yards to follow him on a perfectly harmless spree that lasted several days. The woman's screams triggered a series of phone calls, and the police arrived and actually approached the melee of kids and dogs with guns drawn. Because of the children, and for no other reason, I am certain, no shots were fired. Mack's owner arrived and took his pet home. The other dogs, cuddled and scolded, were carried off the field, and the kids finally settled back down to their ball game.

Things were never the same with Mack after that. Kids donated half their sandwiches as they passed. Hands were thrust through the fence, and Mack wiggled himself silly with the attention he got. Every morning and every afternoon he waited for his friends to come by. On Saturdays and Sundays we often went over just to see Mack. He began getting a tad chubby on peanut butter and jelly and bologna, and his owner could be seen watching from behind a lace curtain. Strangely, I don't think he felt he had gained status by Mack's now universal acceptance in the town. He may, in fact, have lost a little. No one seemed to know very much about him except the man who owned the hardware store, who said he bought an awful lot of tools and hardware supplies. No one knew what he did in that house, but outside of it he seemed to have lost a little something in his walk. He wasn't very fearsome himself, although he was very large. Mack made him fearsome, which is why, I am sure, he never did anything to dispel the terrifying mystique that had grown up around his dog. Mystique grows easily in small towns. Mack, I heard long after we had moved away, lived to a ripe old age and never lost his touch with the kids heading to and from Central Grammar School. The Boston terrier that Mack was presumed to have eaten eventually bit some kid. There had been a rabies scare a few weeks before when a wildly yapping dog had been shot on a landing on the school's staircase while kids huddled with their teachers behind closed classroom doors. The police finally got to shoot their dog, but it wasn't Mack. It was some unknown passer-through desperately ill with a dread disease more commonly encountered then than now. The Boston terrier, however, was put to sleep, and the extraordinarily mean old lady died shortly after that. Mack, wiggling his husky, muscled bottom to the end, outlived them all. I have always considered this story one of the nicer memories of my childhood in Methuen.

In the rough border country between Scotland and England (rough terrain and a rough history), several forms of terriers evolved. There in the Cheviot and Teviotdale Hills wandered the author Sir Walter Scott. He gathered his notes and impressions, and one of his books, published in 1814, was called *Guy Mannering*. In that novel there is a farmer named Dandie Dinmont. The character is said to have been fashioned after a real farmer named James Davidson who lived in Hindlee, near Hawick, and who was known to Scott. The character Dandie Dinmont had six distinctive dogs: Auld Pepper, Auld Mustard, Young Pepper, Young Mustard, Little Pepper, and Little Mustard. In time that terrier type was recognized as a breed called the Dandie

Dinmont terrier, the only dog, as far as I know, named after a fictional character. I suppose we could also call it the James Davidson terrier, but Dandie Dinmont it is, eleven inches tall and up to twenty-four pounds in weight, a smart, low-built little gamester with a topknot that immediately marks it wherever it is seen, which isn't many places. It is one of the least often encountered of all the terrier breeds in the United States. There are people who will tell you the Dandie is a breed that is not always reliable with strangers and children. I am one of those people. They can be sweet, but they can also be a bit too quick on the draw.

Today the smooth and wire fox terriers (*not* "wire-haired") have the same standards except for their coats. The smooth was popular only a couple of decades ahead of the wire, and up until not too many years ago the two varieties were interbred. That is no longer done, and the dogs are kept well apart to perpetuate that very important coat difference. The wire hair should never be woolly or silky. The coat should be, as its name implies, harsh and terrier-like, wiry.

Although their standards are identical today on all other points, the two fox terriers probably arose from different backgrounds, and that at least as far back as the eighteenth century. By 1790 a white smooth-coated version of the breed was appearing in paintings. The wire probably came from the original black-and-tan terrier, which was rough-coated. The greyhound, beagle, and some form of bull terrier probably went into the construction of the smooth. Wherever they came from, and that will always remain a mystery, the smooth fox terrier and the wire fox terrier today are, in most people's minds, the prototypes of terrier-kind. They have the spirit, the energy, the disposition, and the high style that define the word "terrier" itself.

When I was growing up, back in the '30s and '40s, terriers were very much more popular than now. I don't know why that is so, because terriers have everything most people need in a dog today. They are among the world's best watchdogs, and they come in a terrific variety of smaller sizes and so are ideal for an apartment or small suburban house. Yet this is not their time. Not so forty years ago. Like half the people we knew, or so it seemed, we owned a wire fox terrier. Ours must have been made of exotic metals of some kind. He could jump higher and remain airborne longer than any dog I have ever known. He could wear sixteen kids down in the playground and still keep going.

When I was five my younger brother was born (putting me in that least enviable of all positions, the middle kid). Bozo took charge at once. When my brother's carriage was put out in the front yard where he could get "the air," no one, no human being, no dog or cat, was permitted to pass by on the sidewalk. Even my father coming home from work was forbidden to approach the carriage to look at his latest son. The mailman stood on the sidewalk across the street and whistled and called until our housekeeper came out muttering and wiping her hands on her apron to cross the street and collect our allotment. That was a twice-a-day routine back then, believe it or not. In fact, Mabel Sarah Helena Moore liked dogs and was glad to have Bozo on duty outside so she could get her work done inside.

Bozo was a typical terrier, possessive, loyal, tough, and unchangeable once he had determined what his role in life was meant to be. His life was ended prematurely by a passing car, and his equal never really appeared in our lives again. Alas, the little boy he guarded so faithfully never even got to know him. The overlap in their lives was too brief. But Bozo knew him, and that was what mattered.

In the agricultural country along the Scottish-English border a little fifteen-inch terrier is often encountered, a denizen of the Cheviot Hills where the Dandie Dinmont is said to have originated. It is a breed seldom seen here, the border terrier. It is an amazing little dog in a number of ways. It is one of the very oldest terrier types, it undoubtedly played a major role in the construction of most modern terriers, it is lively and smart and has a face that says *I am dog,* yet it is just about the least-known terrier in this country and, indeed, over much of England. There is no rational explanation for its not being far more popular than it is, and that has apparently always been the case. Whatever it is that makes one breed catch on and another not is a function of human taste for which there is simply no accounting. Because of its size, "cute" face, and gay disposition, the border terrier should be very popular. Perhaps one day it will be.

In 1973 the American Kennel Club added the name "soft-coated wheaten terrier" to the Terrier Group, and the dog has been growing in popularity ever since. The soft, silky, open gold-wheat coat of this gay Irishman is distinctive. No other dog has a coat or a color quite like it.

Ireland had played an important role in the development of the whole Terrier Group. The kerry blue terrier and the Irish terrier, of course, are distinctly Irish, but just as stock for them flowed from England and Scotland—and Wales— so did Irish ideas flow back into the mainstream of terrier development. Although its origins are lost in the cynological mists, the soft-coated wheaten terrier is an Irish happening. Owners say it is a gift from the gods. It is indeed a joyful dog.

South or southwestern Ireland seem likely for the soft-coated wheaten's place of origin. What seems unlikely is that the afghan hound played a role in its evolution. It has often been suggested, but almost surely isn't so. The afghan was not known in Ireland, as far as we know, when the wheaten was coming into being. It was far away chasing leopards and other distinctly un-Irish game.

In 1864 a Mr. W. C. Bennet was writing about what was unmistakably the wheaten. There is a famous painting called *The Aran Fisherman's Drowned Child.* A Mr. Bacon executed it as an engraving in 1843, and that melancholy scene pictures a wheaten, clearly, looking at the dead child with deep family-dog concern. Very often dogs put in paintings as a bit of local color are just about the only record we have of extinct ancestral breeds and our only way of establishing breed age. Art is history, just as the dog is.

In 1785 there were a lot of wheatens in County Kerry, where they were highly regarded. Tradition has a shipwreck occurring in Tralee Bay. It is a story not at all unlike the one used to account for the Chesapeake Bay retriever in this country. In the Tralee Bay incident the sole survivor is said to have been a powerful blue dog that managed to swim ashore in the heavy seas. In time it gained a reputation for being an immensely successful fighter and was bred to a number of wheaten bitches owned by local people. From that breeding is said to have come the kerry blue terrier, which in fact is probably a younger breed than the wheaten. The story could well be true.

The history of the dog is like that. Shipwrecks, Jack London stories scattered through a matrix of fantasy, ignorance, and splendid scholarship. It is all in the pot together. You believe what you want, accept what you can, give your prejudices their day, and then realize it isn't all that important as long as you are loving your dog and being loved back. Still, the soft-coated wheaten terrier is a fascinating and handsome breed new to the American scene.

And so the terriers go. The cairn and the Skye from the Isle of Skye, the Irish from, of course, Ireland, the Welsh from Wales, the Scottish from Scotland—it seems as if every corner of the British Isles had its favorite breed, and they have come down to us today with their history written in their names as well as in their standards of perfection. Only three breeds in the Terrier Group originated *in present form* outside of the British Isles, and at least two of them do trace back there.

The Australian terrier (like but not to be confused with the silky terrier, a toy) obviously comes from Australia. Originally called the Australian rough, it is descended, it appears certain, from the Scottish, cairn, Dandie Dinmont, Irish, and Yorkshire terriers. That certainly takes it back home to terrier country. The silky terrier, another Australian breed, is down from the Yorkshire. The American Staffordshire terrier, of course, traces back to original English fighting stock. All terriers except one, then, go home to England at some point in their history. What there is about the terriers that so pleases the English character is hard to say, but the people of the British Isles and Ireland have always been the world's leading terrier fans.

The one exception to the British-Irish origin of terrier dogs is the miniature schnauzer. The other two schnauzers known in America, the standard and the giant, are in the Working Group. Only the miniature is placed among the terriers. It is not terrier at all, but probably in part poodle, in part heavy-coated northern spitz, and in part heaven alone knows what. It is an old breed, back to the 1400s at least, and is not part of the same line as the working schnauzers. Time, taste, and manipulation have made the three breeds resemble each other in everything but size.

With all but one of the twenty-three breeds of British

origin, the terriers are the most homogeneous dogs of all. The same hot blood, the same incredible energy, speed, style, and sense of fun, runs through the entire roster like a leitmotiv. Some terriers, the kerry blue and the descendants of the English pit dogs, our dogs of guilt, can be tricky with other animals and should be kept out of trouble by knowledgeable owners, and a few of the terriers do tend to be sharp with people. The scottie, a lovely dog within the family, may be less than pleased to have to deal with strangers. Although they are cuter than cute as puppies, they may decide as adults to try the occasional ankle of someone they consider an intruder. That is not inevitable, it is just the way things go with more than a few examples of the breed. Biting is not unknown with Skye terriers and bedlingtons. This is not a comment meant to disparage your favorite breed or to take away from any breed's glory, but it is common knowledge among judges, groomers, and handlers that with bedlingtons, Skyes, and Dandie Dinmonts you ask first, then touch. It is not an unreasonable rule of etiquette.

On the subject of disposition, biting, stubbornness, or any other area of potential trouble, a point must be made, and since I have just suggested that several breeds may produce biters more than occasionally, this would seem a logical place to make that point. Dogs vary enormously in disposition and intelligence, far more than many people realize. The only serious bite I have ever received was from a breed that is known to virtually never bite. It was a Newfoundland. When I was a kid working in a veterinary hospital, my boss once asked me to get a big Newfy up onto the examining table. (He was wrong in that. He should have kneeled down, since he knew the dog was in pain.) I walked toward the dog, and perhaps it was my white clinic coat, perhaps it was my after-shave, perhaps it was the color of my eyes (old-telephone-pole brown), but the dog took exception to me and bit me badly on my arm. Actually it was a good thing he did, since my arm was at that moment protecting my throat against the thrust of his enormous weight.

It would be foolish for me to take that incident and extend it and say that Newfoundlands are tricky. They are not. They are calm and affectionate, among the most reliable of all dogs. I got a sick animal on a bad day and set up bad vibes and bear the scar now. However, reputations have been built on no more evidence than this.

I was bitten by a collie while judging a match show at a church benefit. Collies are not biters, generally. This one had just had surgery and was sore. I inadvertently touched it in the wrong place. The point is that any nonbiting dog can bite and any somewhat touchy breed will regularly produce dogs that would never bite. I have known scotties that were ridiculously gregarious and loving as adults, but that is not typical. As a rule, though, most terriers are to be watched with other dogs, for they do love a scrap. That is terrier character. Most terriers are wonderful with people and make the best of companions under any conditions. They are small enough for the apartment, frisky enough for the suburban home, and tough enough on vermin to be useful on the farm.

The west highland white terrier, a dog some people think of as the "white scottie," does arise from the same roots as the darker dog. The breed arose in Poltalloch, Scotland. Presumably they appeared before the reign of James I (1603–25) and were known as "earth dogges of Argyleshire." Other names used for the breed one can encounter in older writings are Poltalloch terrier and Roseneath terrier. Roseneath is an estate in Dumbartonshire, Scotland, that belonged to the Duke of Argyll. The west highland white, or westy, as it is almost universally known, came from a tonier background than some of its fellows.

I have known people to criticize virtually every breed of dog for one reason or another, most often personal prejudice. I have never heard anyone knock the westy. Anyone who has been exposed to it is almost certain to love it. For sheer brass, for assertive personality, for insistent involvement, the westy is quite simply one of the nicest dogs in the world. Its only failing may occur if it has to compete with small children for attention.

Friends of ours owned a westy named Tiger. He was an incredible character whose joy of all joys consisted of picking pockets. Peter, our friend, would sit on a chair and allow just the corner of his handkerchief to hang out. Tiger would close in on the bait and very carefully reach up and grab the bit of cloth and be gone, pleased as punch with his accomplishment. I don't know how many thousands of times that game was played, but Tiger never got tired of it.

It was decided that our friends would come to spend a weekend at our country place, and Tiger loomed fairly large as a potential problem. He was a terrier, and we had not only dogs aplenty but cats. It was assumed that Tiger hated cats, because there was one that appeared outside the gate of his yard and taunted him. Tiger would growl, snarl, and bark himself into a near fit whenever the cat appeared to sit inches away from his nose and wash itself. Cats are like that. If they can get to you (or a dog), trust them to do it.

It was arranged that our guests would arrive with Tiger, and if it became clear he couldn't adjust, our veterinarian would board him until it was time for our friends to leave.

On Saturday morning they appeared, and Tiger looked

around at the cats and dogs, shrugged, settled in, and that was that. No trouble with the other dogs, no problem at all with cats, and a little pocket-picking for recreation. Tiger had a lovely weekend. Terriers are like that. You can anticipate all kinds of problems that never arise.

Another memory of mine connected with Tiger may illustrate one of the deeper realities of dog-owning.

Peter's career eventually took them to Amsterdam. A short time ago I routed one of my own trips through Amsterdam so that we could have a reunion.

This must be seen in context, now. Peter is an international financial expert; his wife, Jackie, is an authority on antiques and is an important dealer in their new home. They have an interest in the international wine market and own vineyards in South Africa, and Peter is an extremely advanced opera buff. The point to all this is that they are sophisticated people, hardly wanting for friends, long and happily married, with a life full of the best things, travel, art, and diversity. Yet when I asked about Tiger they saddened and told me that I had missed him by several months. He had died a dog full of his years. We talked about him for a long time, there in front of a great picture window overlooking a picturesque Dutch canal, in a room superbly ornamented with fine art and choice antiques. We sipped an excellent wine while opera played softly on a magnificent stereo set behind us. We spoke of a dog that had brought joy and companionship to people, a dog that had traveled around the world, a dog that had given and gotten the greatest of all the world's commodities, love. The setting, the sophistication of the people, the whole ambience lacking as it was any kind of pretension or shoddiness, seemed to elevate the whole concept of the companion dog. It was just right, just on the right level for Tiger the westy to be remembered ever so fondly by some very nice people indeed.

We have not discussed all of the terriers in detail here, as indeed we can look only briefly at representatives of each group to stress the enormous variety that has been built into the domestic dog. But we have, I hope, given some indication of the terriers, a uniquely consistent group of superior companion animals.

The fifth group is the Toy Group, fifteen breeds for the records, but seventeen in the show ring. That two-breed discrepancy is not difficult to explain. For registration purposes all three sizes of poodle—the toy, miniature, and standard—are listed together. In shows the miniature and standard are shown in the Nonsporting Group and the toy in the Toy Group. The standards for all three sizes of poodle are exactly the same except for size. The toy Manchester terrier accounts for the other half of the discrepancy. It is a toy version of the Manchester terrier, with the same standards except for size and ear style. The toy version's ears may not be cropped. The standard variety's ears frequently are cropped in the United States, but not in England, where cropping is illegal.

With the addition of the toy poodle and the toy Manchester terrier, the seventeen breeds in the Toy Group in America today are:

Affenpinscher   Chihuahua
Brussels Griffon   English Toy Spaniel

Italian Greyhound	Pomeranian
Japanese Chin	Pug
Maltese	Shih Tzu
Miniature Pinscher	Silky Terrier
Papillon	Toy Manchester Terrier
Pekingese	Toy Poodle
	Yorkshire Terrier

The toy dogs, no less than the herding and guard dogs, are dogs with work to do. They have been bred since ancient times to keep people happy. That is their assignment, that is all they are meant to do. Ask any toy; it can be hard work.

"Ancient times" should be qualified. The first Yorkshire terrier ever shown was exposed to the public scrutiny in 1861 at Leeds in England. The year 1861 may not be ancient, but another toy, the maltese, traces back to the Roman occupation of Malta between one and two thousand years before Christ, at least, and probably further back than that. The Romans were on Malta well along in Maltese history. The Phoenicians were there in 3700 B.P. and other Mediterranean races at least a couple of millennia before that. Just when the maltese evolved cannot be determined.

The Italian greyhound, as noted, does go back to Pompeii before the rain of ash from Vesuvius wiped the city out in A.D. 79 and probably was there much earlier than that. The papillon or French butterfly dog is a kind of miniature spaniel down from Spanish breeds of venerable lineage. But the breed itself may be no more than five hundred years old.

The toys, then, vary in age and come from a great many places. The idea of having dogs for companionship can generally be attributed to the upper classes of a great many cultures. Toys have not been the typical dog of the working classes through most of their history. With this group, elitist as it has been before quite modern times, it is interesting to chart its origins.

BREED	LAND OF ORIGIN	PERIOD OF ORIGIN
Affenpinscher	Europe	At least 1600s
Brussels Griffon	Probably Belgium	At least 1600s
Chihuahua	Mexico and Asia	Before 1800 in Mexico; perhaps very far back in Asia
English Toy Spaniel	Japan and China, in all likelihood	In England since at least the 1400s; probably a very ancient breed
Italian Greyhound	Mediterranean	Ancient—Rome or earlier
Japanese Chin	Probably China	Ancient
Maltese	Mediterranean, probably Malta	Ancient
Miniature Pinscher	Germany and Scandinavia	16th or 17th century
Papillon	Spain and Italy	15th or 16th century
Pekingese	China	Ancient
Pomeranian	Scandinavia	Very old, but in present size only a couple of centuries

Pug	China (*not* Holland)	Ancient
Shih Tzu	Tibet or Byzantium	Probably quite ancient; not really known
Silky Terrier	Australia (U.K. stock)	Early 20th century
Toy Manchester Terrier	England	19th century
Toy Poodle	Europe	Unknown
Yorkshire Terrier	England	19th century

The toy poodle, the toy Manchester terrier, the pomeranian, the Yorkshire terrier, and the Italian greyhound were bred down from very well-known types, some of which are still with us (the Manchester terrier, the poodles, and the greyhound), to become toys. All the toys, of course, were genetically engineered down, for they are much smaller than that doggy dog of universal recognition, the beast we might call protodog. All were designed to please people who often had a great deal of leisure. One possible mistake because of names: just as the miniature schnauzer is not a small version of either of the larger schnauzers except incidentally by appearance, the miniature pinscher is not a bred-down version of the doberman. It is, in fact, very much older than the doberman, in all likelihood three or four hundred years older.

As I have explained previously, the Asians, particularly Asian royalty, favored diminutive sleeve dogs, dogs that could actually be carried around in voluminous sleeves. As the chart suggests, the chihuahua, English toy spaniel, Japanese chin, pekingese, pug, and shih tzu probably all originated in relatively ancient times in Tibet and China. They were symbols of voluptuous affluence and counted for much more than people did at the time they were being evolved and for centuries afterward.

The chihuahua is something of a problem dog, far too much problem for so small a beast. This tiny dog was owned by the Toltecs, we assume, in the eighth or ninth century. There is a claim that a dog known as the techichi was indigenous to the land bridge between North and South America. Indigenous can mean "living or growing in a place or condition" (such as climate), but it generally is taken to mean "native to," that is, "originating in." If the techichi or the chihuahua is really native to Central America we are in big trouble on the origin of the dog. Clearly a Middle Eastern wolf didn't give rise to a Central American animal unless it was carried there by artificial means. Tectonic plates and continental drift to the contrary notwithstanding, the dog didn't get to the New World on its own. The techichi, and therefore the chihuahua, originated somewhere else and was transported perhaps as a shipboard companion (across the Atlantic) or was carried on a very long overland journey from Asia via Alaska and the vanished land bridge we know was there. That bridge alone can account for the horse in Asia and Europe (after it had originated in North America) and for man himself, who came eastward to the western world from Asia. (Although that is now open to question.) The chihuahua was a migrating dog one way or the other. The direction it traveled and when it did it are entirely conjectural. Man was in the Amazon Basin at least ten thousand years ago. One further possibility is that the chihuahua's predecessors arrived across the Pacific in reed boats. Once again, if we could really trace dogs and their movements we would know a great deal more about human prehistory. Dogs have been companions of man since the dog's beginnings. They didn't drift around the world on their own—they were carried, abandoned, buried, eaten, and bred. Their movements are the movements of ancient man.

The pug is the largest of all the toys and would seem to belong with the French bulldog and the Boston terrier in the so-called Nonsporting Group. By some marvelous flurry of illogic the pug, at eighteen pounds or more, is a toy while the Boston terrier, at fifteen pounds or less, is a nonsporting breed.

We have owned only one pug in our family, Winnie the Pooh, and he did us a very dirty turn. Winnie was resident at the same time a joyous little toy poodle named Bridgette was alive. They were very good friends, and since Bridgette had come to us as an adult we apparently assumed that she had been spayed. If I recall correctly, and this was some time ago, we had been told that was the case. At any rate, the years passed and Winnie took no special interest in Bridgette at different times of the year. They were just friends. Nothing untoward ever happened in our presence, and both dogs, being toys and born companions, were generally in view.

Then it happened. She gave no signs to warn us, but there was the proof. Bridgette made a nest in the bottom of the linen closet and gave birth to two puppies. Think, now, of a cross between a poodle and a pug. Puggles, poogles, call them what you want, but never in all of the history of the dog has there been a worse combination, at least aesthetically. To this day I can't really describe what they looked like. Watermelon in shape, a semi-corkscrew tail more swinelike than canine, wispy black fur that again came off the dog like small corkscrews, semi-pushed-in faces, ears that stood halfway up, eyes rather too large. Everything about them was halfway there. Our housekeeper took one puppy and a young artist and his wife the other. Both had fine lives in loving homes. I have never seen homelier dogs in my life, but they were loved, and that is what counts. As a worker in the humane movement fighting all my life to get people to spay and neuter their dogs, I was terribly embarrassed by the whole episode. Winnie was clearly unconcerned. He had gotten what he wanted, and as for Bridgette, she took it as she took everything else in life, in stride. She was spayed as soon as it was safe for her to face surgery, and we would have liked to forget the whole thing ever happened except for years we kept getting reports on how well those ugly, ugly little puppies were doing and what lovely, but ugly, dogs they had become. Since that humiliating experience, I have never been able to dispel a suspicion that pugs are sex fiends. I know it is not fair, but who says life has to be fair? Pugs may not in fact be sex fiends, but given the number of them that are around today they must be doing something right.

Just as the traditional fanciers of toys have often been considered somewhat effete, the dogs themselves have often been referred to as somehow lesser creatures of a different kind. That is macho nonsense and not at all true to the spirit of dogdom. Anyone who thinks either is true exhibits personal hang-ups, not cynological savvy. There is no dog in any group that is doggier than a toy Manchester terrier, a better watchdog than a miniature pinscher, or more assertive than the papillon. The other toys are in their own way, to their own degree, tough, rough, assertive, pushy, brassy, demanding, rewarding, hardheaded bullies. The people who own them are the same way, each after his or her own fashion. In our household, large dogs are the general rule. We have bloodhounds, a golden retriever, a Siberian husky, and various other animals at the moment and have had at least seven or eight other breeds and lots of random-breds. The biggest character we ever had was that wanton toy poodle bitch, Bridgette. Bridgette or Biddy, in her day, which alas has ended, absolutely demanded center stage and got it on her own terms. It is true that she was easier to have in your lap than a 140-pound bloodhound, but that made her not one whit less a dog. When I hear macho remarks from the owners of German shorthaired pointers or briards that are designed as much to say *See what a man I am* as they are to mar the reputation of a breed, I smile. If they only knew. I suspect many of them do. I strongly believe there are a great many closet toy lovers among them. On such thin threads manhood (and womanhood) may dangle.

It is quite true that the mysterious, confounding chihuahua is a tad spindly for our life-style. Our house of thundering hounds and heavy human foot traffic would not be the best setting for a dog of such fine bone construction, but that is a practical matter, not a disparagement of the breed or the people who fancy it. All hail the chihuahua and its owner. The chihuahua's family history, given sufficient scope, is more intriguing than that of most people I know. At least we know how our ancestors got here, when, and where they came from.

The most ferocious little character we ever owned is a toy. He is still alive, but he is dwelling elsewhere. We speak of him as being away at camp.

The very old dwarf spaniel we call papillon today gets

its newer name from the French word for "butterfly." The little spaniel derivative does have a spread of ear that is reminiscent of a butterfly when seen from behind. It is a toy in every way, especially traditionally, for it was the darling of European royalty. It is often stated with pride by papillon fanciers that Madame de Pompadour had two (Mimi and Inez), Marie Antoinette liked them a lot, and the Queen of Poland fancied them as well. For a time, so did I.

When my great and good friend Biddy the toy poodle had to be sent to the great kennel beyond, my wife and kids decided I needed a toy of my own. Buckeroo the papillon was presented on my birthday and was renamed Tigger for no particular reason. Tigger had certain problems. He was tough. Bloodhounds weighing more than thirty times as much as he did were regularly set to yelping, Tigger hanging off their flues growling like *Tyrannosaurus rex* with a toothache. Even the mailman was seen scurrying down the long driveway with a papillon firmly attached to his ankle. To this day he won't come back down the drive despite the promise of substantial Christmas recognition.

On one occasion I emerged from the deep, dark, dank dungeon where I write my books to make myself a cup of coffee. I drifted idly to the cheese drawer in the refrigerator and no sooner had begun to eye the neatly wrapped packages lying there when I was surrounded by a herd of dogs. They know. And dogs do like a bit of cheese in the afternoon. I cut myself a wedge of promising-looking Colby and cut another slab to divide into cubes and pass around to the ever faithful. Each dog took his prize off to savor in whatever privacy could be found. I was completing my small kitchen tasks when I heard a strange sound from just outside the kitchen door. Tracing it to its source, I found poor little Tigger the papillon lying on his side flailing his legs in great distress. Very foolishly I had not properly considered his size when I gave him his cube of cheese, and he had gulped it down because of the presence of all the other dogs. It had lodged in his throat and he was beginning to slow down when I found him. He was near death.

It wasn't difficult to figure out what had happened. I scooped Tigger up and rammed my finger down his throat. The cheese was dislodged instantly and the tiny dog gulped in the sweet air of survival. He looked up at me, and I could see the terror melt away in his eyes. He was unresisting, and I carried him to a cushion in front of the fireplace and gently put him down. He was exhausted. He obviously needed to sleep. I watched him for a minute or so and, satisfied that his breathing was quite regular, I went back to the kitchen. A few minutes later I came back with my coffee and a cheese sandwich. I put them down and went over to check once again on Tigger. I knelt beside his cushion and ever so gently ran my hand down his side. The little bastard bit me.

A regular visitor to our home is a lady then known as Mrs. Marilyn Miller, or T to her friends. She is a hopeless dog lover and always had a Yorkshire terrier in hand. Dirty Face, the first of her yorkies we knew, died and was replaced with an even smaller one, Macy, the world's most nearly microscopic dog. Macy and Tigger fell in love, and Tigger transferred that love to T. After every visit of mother and dog, Tigger would go into a steep decline, curling up near the front door and crying far into the night. In time Tigger began going for visits, and there he lives to this day. T eventually married cartoon genius Charles Addams of *The*

New Yorker, who brought his pet, Alice B. Curr, to live at Toad Hall, one of the homes he and T now share. (They were married in a pet cemetery, T wearing black to be cheerful.) When we visit Charles and T, Tigger growls ferociously at me to remind me that he is never coming home again. He and Macy are together forever, the two of them not weighing as much as a coil of sweet Italian sausage between them. Tigger and Charles have worked out a relationship I was never able to develop. I think there is a touch of the Addams humor in Tigger. I feel that if he ever grew large he would become a science fiction movie star in Japan. He would eat whole cows, horses, and people and pick his teeth with Masai spears. Anyone who thinks of the papillon as less a dog than any other breed is operating from a base of puréed nonsense.

The Caras household seems to require the presence of at least one assertive, diminutive dog. Once Tigger had gone to grace what is now the Addams household, Piggy came, as a Christmas gift. Piggy is a Jack Russell terrier, an unrecognized breed I will discuss in the next chapter. Another JRT, Annie, followed. But, in seeking balance, our house, which is a country house, is a satisfactory habitat for a good many animals and always has its share of giants (bloodhounds), reasonably large dogs (a golden, the husky), and a few beasts to represent the random-bred line of canine development. It also needs one small character or two to put all of the others in their place and keep them there. A toy poodle did it for years, a papillon until he fell hopelessly in love with Macy the yorkie, and now it is the pair of Jack Russells, toy-sized terriers of special distinction. Toys are dogs through and through, and don't ever let anyone with a tattoo on the back of his hand, a good horse, and a cool look tell you different. Most toys could and would with joy put a horse to flight, at least any horse with half a horse's brain.

✋   ✋

And now that confounding group, number six, the Nonsporting Group. Currently, there are eleven breeds listed in dogdom's catch-all. There is no particular character to the group, although it contains some perfectly splendid breeds. It is the place you put a breed when it doesn't *seem* to go anyplace else. The problem is that so many more dogs belong in it, and as we have suggested it could well be called the Companion Dog Group, because that is just what it contains. Its members may all have had very different purposes once upon a time. The Nonsporting Group today consists of:

Bichon Frise	French Bulldog
Boston Terrier	Keeshond
Bulldog	Lhasa Apso
Chow Chow	Poodle
Dalmatian	Schipperke

Tibetan Terrier

It is my feeling that the following breeds should also be in this group of companion dogs:

	Now
Basenji	Hound
Cocker Spaniel	Sporting
Dachshund	Hound
Miniature Schnauzer	Terrier
Norwegian Elkhound	Hound
Pug	Toy

What about the breeds presently in the Nonsporting Group? A rare mixture of history and taste. A veritable United Nations of the dog world. This is where they came from and possibly when:

BREED	LAND OF ORIGIN	PERIOD OF ORIGIN
Bichon Frise	Mediterranean region	Ancient times, resurgence after 14th century
Boston Terrier	New England	19th century
Bulldog	England	Possibly 12th century or earlier
Chow Chow	China	Very ancient almost certainly; easily before Christ
Dalmatian	Not known	Not known—old!
French Bulldog	England	18th to 19th centuries
Keeshond	Arctic then Holland	17th century or earlier
Lhasa Apso	Tibet	Ancient
Poodle	Unknown	Unknown
Schipperke	Belgium	Late 16th or early 17th century
Tibetan Terrier	Tibet	Ancient—at least pre-Christ

The history of the poodle and the dalmatian are simply lost to us and are probably well beyond recovery. The fluffy little bichon frise arose in a variety of forms at various places around the northern coast of the Mediterranean. Although you would hardly guess it today there is probably some water dog, perhaps water spaniel, in its background. It is usually stated that Spanish seamen introduced the dog to the Canary Islands at least a thousand years ago and that it was rediscovered there in the fourteenth century by Italian sailors and brought back to the mainland, where it gained steadily in favor with the privileged classes. The breed has lived well ever since.

The Boston terrier (not Boston bull) is a true American development, one of the relatively few in the dog world. Almost unquestionably the original cross was between a bulldog from England and an English terrier, probably all white in color. The first Bostons weighed about thirty-two pounds, although the trend is, as earlier noted, toward very much smaller dogs today.

I grew up at a time (from 1928 on) and in a place (near Boston) where almost everyone seemed to own a Boston terrier. They always have been super little companions, and although they were somewhat larger fifty years ago than they are today they still hold a warm place in my heart. They are probably the all-time greatest rubber-ball chasers. My parents had Bostons before they had me, and so did many of my aunts, uncles, and cousins. They were ubiquitous when I came along.

It was no surprise, then, when I first met Jill Langdon Barclay (who was later to become Jill Langdon Barclay Caras) to find that she had a Boston terrier. That made her, obviously, a perfectly normal person. Pixie was like every other Boston I ever knew—you couldn't be in the house two minutes without a pink rubber ball suddenly appearing between your feet and anxious eyes meeting your own. Very shortly after Jill and I were married her parents were off on a trip (perhaps to get over the shock I gave them by marrying their only daughter), and Pixie was left with us. We got on well: I threw the bloody little pink ball as I was supposed to and walked Pixie, and walked Pixie and walked Pixie. One day I was bringing her back from her walk when she suddenly got it into her head that she should be outside the elevator and not inside. She had grown up in a single-family home and the whole business of living temporarily in New York City and not having a yard and requiring a leash and getting into boxes that lurched and were always in different places when you got out of them seemed to have unnerved poor Pixie, who was by then well along in her years.

At any rate, on this particular occasion she went into reverse without warning. She was such a well-behaved little dog that I had gotten into what proved to be the foolish habit of unhooking her lead as we entered the apartment-house lobby. On this occasion she went into reverse just as the elevator door closed, and as luck would have it her head got caught in the door. Frantically I braced a foot against the wall of the elevator and tugged until I went blue in the face. Pixie was making the most fearful sounds, a combination of gulps, gurgles, wails, and moans. Someone on a floor above was rattling against the door on their floor and no doubt cursing me for holding the elevator in the lobby. I tugged, the box in the shaft lurched, Pixie gurgled and moaned, and finally both Pixie and I fell backward as the door slid free. Pixie promptly threw up on my shoes. Bostons don't always have the steadiest stomachs in the world. She obviously felt I had plotted the whole thing, because she never again would chase a ball if I threw it. She held a grudge. I felt guilty for the longest time, but could never figure out why I should. Boston terriers have peculiar eyes. They give good guilt.

The magnificent bulldog of England was bred for ferociousness and insensitivity to pain—that is, until 1835, when dog combat became illegal in England. Its sequence of ancestry is uncertain, but somewhere way back there had to be mastiff blood. The ferociousness has been bred out of the bulldog, although some still show resentment of other animals. Other dogs should not say rude things to the bulldogs they meet, not unless they have a lot of muscle to back it up. With people, however, there are few more lovable dogs to match this animal of absurd design. Bulldogs have trouble with the heat, have trouble breathing, are veritable methane plants, and as often as not have to be born by caesarian section because of the large size of the puppies' heads. Still, it is an absolutely lovable dog.

Jill and I bought a bulldog in London, favoring the British breeders at the time. Pudge was a rotund appetite on the hoof. There was a very telling note of the English love for this breed before we left. While Pudge was being tidied up for her trip an elderly English lady happened into the room. "Ah, you are making her tidy, are you?" she said to the kennel girl. We were standing off to the side and were not noticed. "Yes, mum, she is going to New York, this one is." "New York! New York, indeed!" huffed the old lady. "Poor dear, she'll not be appreciated there." In fact she was and in fact bulldogs are. Their following here is devoted. They are the fifth most popular breed in the Nonsporting Group.

The chow chow has a history that is about 75 percent conjecture, but China was apparently where it originated as a breed apart and where it was fostered for a very long time.

Its exact age is not known, not even its approximate age, nor is its precise relationship to the other northern spitz types, but they are all related. The geographical spread of the spitz is enormous:

Chow Chow	China
Norwegian Elkhound	Scandinavia
Samoyed	Siberia
Husky	Siberia
Malamute	Alaska
Keeshond	Arctic or subarctic then northern Europe
Pomeranian	Scandinavia
Akita	Japan

While the American Kennel Club does not recognize the spitz as a breed, the United Kennel Club in Kalamazoo does.

The dalmatian is a fine cynological problem, for you would think that so distinctive a dog would have a clear history. That is not the case; no one knows where the breed came from or what it was really intended for originally. It is at least likely hunting figured in somewhere during the breed's evolution. It is a mysterious breed, but one much loved as the coach dog or firehouse dog of today. Dalmatians add flash and style to any situation; there is an undeniable panache about them. Well-marked specimens with spots that are no larger than silver dollars and not touching each other are hard to find. Unfortunately, many dalmatian puppies are born deaf. It is a breed problem, and the prospective owner should check for hearing. A deaf dog can make a perfectly fine pet, but a new owner should know what he or she is getting into.

Certainly the French bulldog is a small version of England's lovely old breed the bulldog. The French say *non* to that and define somewhat vaguely what they call special characteristics to prove different lineage. The large ears and flattened skull are often cited. There was a toy variety of the bulldog in England in the mid-nineteenth century, and it is known that some were sent to France. The English just didn't cotton to it. The French dog is quite different from its English ancestor. It is smaller and a little neater in outline and has a far less ferocious expression. It is as good a companion animal as its ancestor from across the Channel, but its face looks less like an unmade bed. It is very difficult for the French to acknowledge receiving anything from the English except venereal disease and tourists who speak French even more poorly than Americans. Clearly the chauvinistic French cannot admit that they have anything, even a dog, that came from the land of fish and chips.

The keeshond (plural keeshonden) has a remarkable history. By the end of the eighteenth century the keeshond had had several hundred years of popularity in the Netherlands. It is not known to have been a hunter or a working dog of any description, just a friend much admired. In the period immediately before the French Revolution, there was political unrest in Holland as well. The partisans of the Prince of Orange, the Prinsgezinden, were aligned against the Patriotten, lower-to-upper-middle-class followers of a rebel named Kees de Gyselaer. He lived in Dordrecht and was a dog lover, something of a Dutch national characteristic. His dog, Kees, immodestly named for its owner, gave the breed its present name. It became a kind of standard for De Gyselaer's movement, and when that movement was swept away by forces loyal to the prince, the breed became a political liability. It was not a good idea, apparently, with tempers still running high, to walk a dog that was the symbol of a fallen cause. The keeshond or "Kees's dog" all but vanished. We don't know what the dog was called before it became "the dog of the people," but it almost certainly had several hundred years of history on the barges that plied the Rhine River. How it came to the Rhine from the arctic or subarctic, where it certainly originated, is not known, but probably through the Scandinavian countries and possibly via some form of the Norwegian elkhound. All of that will forever remain in the realm of the unknown.

In 1920 the Baroness van Hardenbroek decided to rebuild the keeshond to its former glory, as a dog, not as a political symbol. There turned out to be enough of them living in relative obscurity on the river barges whence they had come so long ago for their brief moment of political glory for the baroness to gather a good strong diversity of bloodlines while still being true to type. She rebuilt her dog. The Dutch Kennel Club (Kynologisch Gebied in Nederland) accepted the standards, and the Dutch Keeshond Club began pushing its breed. The cross to England came soon after, for by 1925 the dog was being admired there and shortly after in the United States as well. The breed is back, its romantic history one more tale to tell.

Once upon a time all small dogs were called terriers, unless they were spaniels or toys, and that is how the Tibetan terrier, one of four distinct breeds from that country, got its name. That is due to size, not lineage or association with the almost exclusively British strain. Long considered a bringer of luck, the breed has been known outside of Asia for only a relatively short time. Its ancestry is as mysterious

as the mountain passes over which it was carried to the
outside world.

The seventh group of dogs recognized by the American
Kennel Club today appeared in 1982 as a splinter group,
the Herding Dogs. Until that time its fourteen members
were part of the Working Dogs group, but that made that
group so unwieldy in the group ring with thirty-two breeds
that the split into Working Dogs and Herding Dogs was
inevitable.

The Herding Dogs, as the new grouping is presently con-
stituted, consists of:

Australian Cattle Dog	Collie (Rough and smooth coated)
Bearded Collie	German Shepherd Dog
Belgian Malinois	Old English Sheepdog
Belgian Sheepdog	Puli
Belgian Tervuren	Shetland Sheepdog
Bouvier des Flandres	Welsh Corgi (Cardigan)
Briard	Welsh Corgi (Pembroke)

There is a singular logic and consistency to this grouping.
These are the dogs of maximum economic significance to
man through the millennia. Without these dogs to aid in the
handling of livestock (or to take the task over completely)
man's lot would have been a far different one. Quite simply,
he could not have managed animals in the numbers he was
required to as his needs grew, his own needs and the demands of commerce.

There is another consistency to this group. Like the working dogs from which they were recently separated, these
dogs, for the most part, have retained original character. It

is true that many breeders do go entirely for style today and ignore original intent, but most or all of the herding dogs could, in a generation or two, be back at work. Their services may never again be in demand over most of the world, but in Scotland, in Australia, and in other areas as well herding dogs still ply their trade with dignity and purpose and to the very great benefit of man.

Not all of the names in this group are as revealing as they might be. But, then, that is true of all of the groups, as we have seen.

"Old English sheepdog" is a misnomer. It is not origin that is at stake, for the breed did originate in the British Isles, probably in the west, Devon, Somerset, and Cornwall. It is that word "old." There are many old English sheepdogs; the collie is probably quite old, although its origin is confusing, because the Scots were terrible record keepers. The cardigan Welsh corgi came to the British Isles, to Wales probably, 3,000 to 3,500 years ago. The pembroke Welsh corgi probably traces its history back a thousand years in the United Kingdom, which was then not a united kingdom at all. The old English sheepdog is probably less than two hundred years old. Its name claims for it that which it cannot really claim for itself, cynological antiquity.

The designation of both the cardigan dog and the pembroke dog as Welsh corgis suggests a relationship that simply does not exist. In A.D. 1107, Henry I invited Flemish weavers to cross the Channel and establish their trade in Wales. They brought their favorite dogs with them, quite probably the ancestors of the pembroke (or tailless) Welsh corgi. Much, much earlier, around 1200 B.C., Celts from Central Europe came to the Welsh hill country and brought the dog that would later be known as the cardigan (with a tail) Welsh corgi. The country where they settled is now known as Cardiganshire. The two dogs have different origins, although both were used as cattle drovers and very clever ones at that.

Allowing that vulgarity is vulgarity only when it is intended to be, I am compelled to tell a story about how I learned (and you will now learn) how to remember which corgi has the tail. Having just read the preceding paragraphs, you know that it is the cardigan, but you will be likely to forget it just as I did for so many years. I was forever checking it out, remembering it for an hour, and forgetting again. I have never been good with faces, and frequently poor with tails.

I was at a dog show, standing at ringside with a veterinarian friend. "Dale," I said, "I have been around dogs all my life and have never been able to remember which corgi has the tail."

"I will help you," my veterinarian friend said, "for I, too, had that problem as a young man. You will never forget again. I can promise you that." I leaned forward, intent, although the veterinarian was twelve years my junior.

"My brother went to a boys' school. Across the street was a girls' school," Dale explained. "He frequently wrote to me complaining that the girls in that girls' school were all homely. The name of that girls' school was Pembroke College. Now you will never forget—pembroke equals no tail." I have never forgotten and have longed for an opportunity to share that with other people who might need it. Now you will never forget. Resent, yes; forget, no.

In this chapter and the one preceding it, it has not been my intention to describe all the breeds of dog we recognize, for that would have been unrealistic. In the United States we recognize only a fraction of the breeds known around the world. What has been my goal is proof of diversity, for if there is anything that matches the miracle of the dog's impression on the life of mankind it is that animal's own almost unbelievable genetic willingness to fit need, taste, style, time, and place. What you ask of the dog as an individual animal or as a species is almost never refused, even if it involves shrinking, shedding coat permanently, and growing a new style of tail. Ask and ye shall receive.

6
Diversity III: The Miscellaneous Breeds and Other Dogs

In the last few years, two new breeds were recognized by the American Kennel Club. One of them, the ibizan hound, is a member of the Hound Group. Like its cousins the greyhound, saluki, and afghan, it is an ancient Middle Eastern coursing hound. The other, the Australian cattle dog, is, quite legitimately, a member of the Working Group. Both dogs have this in common: prior to recognition they had been tucked away in the never-never land of dogdom known as the Miscellaneous Class. Membership in this AKC category means a lot of people are making chirping sounds about wanting to foster the breed, but not enough are really doing it with a good enough studbook to warrant full recognition. Pressure gets a breed, one that is recognized overseas, into the Miscellaneous Class, and even more pressure gets it out. Dogs in that class are seen around but are not allowed to compete for championship points. People in the dog world keep their eye on the class, because sooner or later most members seem to pop out and get recognized. They are often the dog world's future enthusiasms.

As of this writing, seven breeds are in the Miscellaneous Class:

BREED	ORIGIN	PROBABLE AGE
Australian Kelpie	Australia	19th century
Border Collie	British Isles	No later than the 16th century
Cavalier King Charles Spaniel	England and the U.S.	Antique lineage but very recent redevelopment
Miniature Bull Terrier	England	Late 18th, early 19th century
Pharaoh Hound	Egypt, probably	Extremely ancient
Spinone Italiano	Italy	Probably 16th or 17th century
Tibetan Spaniel	Tibet	Ancient and unknown

From that list some breeds will gain recognition and remain relatively obscure while others will soar in popularity. The Australian kelpie, like its compatriot the Australian cattle dog that has just recently been recognized, is a fine, sturdy, and very intelligent working dog. Its history is not behind it; the breed is living out its planned destiny today. Its specialty is sheep, and in fact it is of enormous importance to sheepherders in remote regions of Australia at this moment. Also known as the barb, it is, for Working Group enthusiasts, what dogs are supposed to be all about. At thirty pounds it is a lithe, quick, and very sure dog. It has a shepherd look about it reminiscent of the German and the Belgian dogs of that calling. It is a creature of good balance and workmanlike proportions, but elegance is not its name. It remains to be seen if American fanciers—and it is from them that popularity comes—feel they need another shepherd of this style and size to admire. It is certainly legitimate as a breed. What is missing is a passionate American following of any size.

The border collie, another shepherd that looks the part and is quite unlike the elegant narrow-headed collie we love so much in America today, is bright, agile, and loyal. If a following develops for this breed it is likely to move on to great popularity. It needs a shove to get started. The hardworking border collie may weigh up to forty-five pounds and can stand to eighteen inches at the shoulder. It is a substantial medium-sized dog that comes in a pleasing variety of colors—black, gray, or blue merle, often with white points. Merle, a bluish-gray blotchy pattern, is found in a number of breeds including the collie, Shetland sheepdog, and, as noted, the Australian cattle dog and border collie. It may also be tricolored—black, white, and tan. Collies have been so popular for so long that a new form of collie, one somewhat less refined, might just be welcome with our back-to-the-soil mentality in America today. Dogs, it must not be forgotten, reflect sociological trends, fears, aspirations, fantasies, and needs.

The lovely thing about the border collie is that it carries dogdom back toward original purpose and form. If it had not been for dogs like this one we would not be where we are today. It could have turned out well for us without real working dogs—well but differently. We have depended on livestock to see us through to higher planes of existence, and keeping livestock in any quantity without dogs simply was not practical. Sheepherding people especially needed sheepherding dogs. Whatever the forerunners of today's gussied-up show shepherds may have been, they were like the border collie in drive, intelligence, persistence, and stamina. That and that alone could make this particular breed shine forth in the future. It is in every sense a symbol of the best of the past. With the border collie you get not only a dog but a real living history that has lasted in constant form up to modern times. That is intriguing, and I predict the super-smart border collie will have its day. The very fact that a family can afford to keep a medium-sized dog as a pet represents affluence within that society that has been in part a gift of that dog's forerunners. Wool, weaving, trade in cloth, warmth in winter, mutton and lamb on the table, all available to man because of working dogs of the sheepherding kind.

The cavalier King Charles spaniel is a lead-pipe cinch for recognition. It is the reconstruction of the toy spaniels that appeared in so many paintings from the sixteenth to the eighteenth century. Those spaniels were in modern times altered so badly by breeders of the English toy spaniels that one Roswell Eldridge of Long Island, New York, began hankering for a touch of the original dog. He went to England and found people who shared his theories, and together they rebuilt that old toy spaniel type. They lengthened the muzzle and flattened out the little apple head of the English toy of the twentieth century. They successfully went back in time and in less than half a century had the cavalier King Charles spaniel recognized in England. It is only a matter of time here. The cavalier weighs between thirteen and eighteen pounds and is already showing up at highly publicized social events in the arms of movie stars and other stylistic shakers and movers. We shall see this breed recognized in our time. It is my guess that it will be the next breed recognized in America.

A few years ago I happened to bump into a Hollywood leading lady whose time has definitely come and gone. To a person of my generation, though, the face, the voice, and the name are magic. On this particular day the grand lady of once upon a time had two cavalier King Charles spaniels in her arms, and they obviously meant a great deal to her. I commented on them, as it seemed polite to do, but made the disastrous mistake of not recognizing them or not, at least, paying enough attention to their special qualities. I referred to them as English toy spaniels or Japanese chin, I have forgotten which, but clearly they belonged to neither tribe. Our lady of the dogs, known in her day as a great face slapper as well as a sensuous destroyer of souls beyond comparison, withered me with a stare-down that had dissolved many a leading man into his shoes and advised me that I was displaying abysmal ignorance for a reputed authority on animals. She was quite right, of course, but she could have gone a little softer or made an obscene phone call to me later that day. She didn't *have* to do it in front of my son and several family friends.

The point is that leading ladies, old and forgotten as well as new and arising, are walking around with cavaliers on leash and in arms. That bodes well for the future of the breed. That was the company they were meant to keep—the company of queens.

The miniature bull terrier goes as far back in history as the other former fighting terriers. Again, there is no question about the legitimacy of the breed, it is only a matter of enough people becoming interested in it. It is truly a miniature animal, for it weighs twenty pounds or less, while the bull terrier, although there is no weight specified in its standards, weighs three to four times as much. Without question, the minature bull terrier is clearly all terrier, but it is the size of a toy. On both counts it has considerable appeal.

The pharaoh hound is a fascinating dog. The breed almost surely originated in Egypt six or seven thousand years ago and could be the oldest purebred dog still with us. It certainly challenges the extremely old saluki. It is suggested but hardly proved that Phoenicians carried pharaoh hounds to Malta, where the breed is coveted and guarded and held pure to this day. They are used to course rabbits and are known on their island home as Kalb-tal-Kenek. The first pharaoh hounds seen in England, according to records, appeared there in the 1930s, but it is not known what happened to them. They were seen there again in the early 1960s and in the United States a few years later. There seems to be a following building, and it would seem only just. There is something nice about being able to look at representations five thousand years old to see if your dog fits the mold it should. That does stress the timelessness of man and dog together. A failure to recognize the pharaoh hound eventually could come about only as the result of a faltering in the breed's American following. It would seem an absurd denial of the history of the purebred dog. Since Anubis and the pharaoh hound were undoubtedly the same animal, we have here, in all likelihood, the only breed of dog actually elevated to the rank of a god.

No group is more tradition-bound than the Sporting Group, and dogs are slow to gain recognition on that hallowed list. Fanciers of the sporting breeds are hard on their dogs (not in the sense of cruel, but in the judging of standards) and hard on themselves. A dog has to do more than conform to a list of points, it has to perform to gain a following. There doesn't seem too much doubt, however, that the spinone italiano or Italian pointer will make it eventually. There is obviously hound in the breed, for the ears, although set high, are typical hound ears. This twenty-six-inch, fifty-six-pound double-coated (white or white with yellow or light-brown markings) dog is keen, alert, proven in the field for at least three centuries, and hardy, since it is essentially a breed of northern Italy. It will be fancied here, and almost certainly given recognition. Friends who have lived in Italy come back extolling this breed, saying it is stubborn but superbly intelligent. Once trained it seems to be almost human in its insight and what appears at least to be common sense and good manners.

The Tibetan spaniel, which is no more a spaniel than the Tibetan terrier is a terrier, is bound to become popular with time and active promotional efforts. Nine to fifteen pounds in weight, it is not unlike the pekingese, which may go to fourteen pounds. Whether we need two dogs rather alike of overlapping weights is moot. If enough people like the breed we shall have it, and, indeed, why not? Dogs are to make people happy, and if the clearly misnamed Tibetan spaniel pleases enough people then there should be no power that denies them the pride of full recognition and the right to earn championships and be known by the canine company they keep. There are people, undeniably, that prefer to come in on the ground floor with a breed and be a part of building that breed's standards, style, and popularity. That offers more to them personally than moving in on a breed long established and simply trying to do the next fancier one better by producing a better litter.

But then there are the people who do not care to have

their favorite breed recognized. The fanciers of the Jack Russell terrier have put a little reverse body English on snobbery and turned their backs on the world of organized dog fancying. They have, after all, their horses! And most people who breed and own Jack Russell terriers are horsy.

Parson John Russell developed the Jack Russell terrier early in the nineteenth century, and its popularity was quick in coming. The descendant of basic English terrier stock, really an aberrant fox terrier, the Jack Russell is built low to the ground and is fast on its feet. It was meant, so the story goes, to ride in a kind of saddlebag while its owner rode to the hounds. When the fox or other prey went to earth (burrowed), the feisty little terrier was tossed from the horse and hit the ground running. It followed the object of the hunt to earth and there killed it or was dragged out backward by his typical one-handful terrier tail, dragging the quarry after it.

A great many people who do not ride to hounds today own Jack Russells, and those who know the breed are devoted to them. They are generally owned by people who own other breeds as well.

The Jack Russell is not recognized by the American Kennel Club for the simple reason that its fanciers do not wish recognition. They fancy themselves above it. They do not want their breed to become generally popular. Only recently did breeders in the United Kingdom relent and apply for recognition by the kennel club there. They got it.

The dog fancy that deals with the recognized breeds responds in kind. Mention the Jack Russell and you are likely to get a sniff and a slight turn of the head. There are mumbled comments about the breed's not breeding true, its having several coat lengths and textures, there being too few established standards by which excellence could be assessed. That, of course, is sour grapes. When the Tibetan terrier that isn't a terrier was recognized, no one seemed to know what length or height it should be, and cobby dog vs. elongated dog vied for approval. Yet the breed was recognized. The newest breed on the list, the Australian cattle dog, is nothing if not nondescript, but will one day be as refined as the boxer or the collie. The dachshund comes in a variety of sizes and coat styles. The Norwich terrier, before it was divided into Norwich and Norfolk terriers, had ears that might go in either of two directions, up or down, and neck length was not clearly established, which is why two breeds had to be made out of one here as it is in England.

To deny the potential of the Jack Russell terrier is to overlook the history of dogs. How much evolution is supposed to take place before recognition and how much after is apparently the only question upon which people could disagree. A stroll through the AKC offices at 51 Madison Avenue in New York treats one to an impressive collection of dog paintings, bequests to the registry that come in every year. A review of those paintings shows just how much evolution has taken place among recognized breeds over the years, and even within memory the German shepherd and the Boston terrier, to name two obvious breeds, have had whole lines suffer terribly at the hands of some breeders seeking masses of puppies to sell above all other considerations.

The Jack Russells, true to original nature and intent, are fine farm dogs. They are fine in a house of any size and ideal in an apartment. They are super watchdogs and do tend toward the yappy side of the street. That has to be curbed, as does their natural tendency to treat everything as fair game. Improperly conditioned Jack Russells, despite the fact that they are toy-sized, can become cat killers. The two Jack Russells that now live with us and the one that lives with a friend nearby are all cat lovers. They have to be raised knowing what is expected and what is allowed and what behavior means the end of the world. They are clowns, lovers, watchdogs, pals, and tyrants, everything a little terrier should be.

A startling breed has suddenly, in the late 1970s and early 1980s, sprung into view after very nearly dropping into that great pit of extinction that swallows wildlife species and domestic breeds alike. The Chinese pronounce it *sah-pay* (there is no plural form in Chinese) and we call it shar-pei. It looks like a miniature hippopotamus with badly fitting panty hose, all over. This wrinkled Asian wonder goes back nearly two thousand years, as far as we can tell, but in recent years was reduced to scattered remnants. It has generally been referred to as the rarest dog in the world, but with no more authority than the *Guinness Book of Records*.

Apparently, the southern part of China, along the coast of the South China Sea, was the traditional home of the breed. It was a dog of the peasant farmer and acted as house guard, flock protector, and general hunting dog, with a flair for wild boar. That was a tough assignment for a dog that weighs a half a hundredweight. Pottery from the Han Dynasty (202 B.C.–A.D. 220) represents this breed well, quite like the dog we know today. In at least one collection the figurine is referred to as a China tomb dog, that sepulchral name apparently suggesting the statuette was made and placed to protect the dead as the living dog had the living person. Some researchers suggest the dog was principally a hunting dog used on mongoose. Since people kept mongooses to combat cobras, which are also common in southern China, the story becomes problematical.

According to stories, the shar-pei was not a fighting dog during the reign of the Han. Later, though, in Kwangtung Province, gambling and gaming of all kinds got out of hand and dogfights were extremely popular. The tough shar-pei became something of a favorite in the pits, and their reputation as primarily a fighting dog was established.

The characteristics that mark the shar-pei today apparently stemmed from those days in the fighting arena. They have loose skin that is difficult to hold on to—at least, the dog inside that skin is hard to hold. It is bristly, which, one could project, is less than terrific in the mouth. And the shar-pei have recurved canine teeth, which must be less than terrific to have embedded in your flesh.

As China began opening up to the West, other fighting dogs were introduced. The mastiff and the bulldog at least were imported, and the shar-pei began losing its theretofore seemingly unchallengeable status with the breeders in the village of Dah Let, the principal center of fighting-dog breeding. By the time the communists took over in China the shar-pei was in deep trouble, as were all dogs not being raised for food. By the 1970s the breed was on what appeared to be the final decline. A tax had been levied on all companion dogs in 1947, with the justification that they were decadent, bourgeois luxuries. That attitude is not too surprising in a culture where dogs were (1) eaten, (2) fancied by impossibly cruel potentates everyone was trying to forget (except for the priceless art treasures they caused to be created), and (3) probably put at the breasts of wet nurses whose babies, if we are to believe the tales, were killed to make room for the emperor's sleeve dogs.

At any rate, the bourgeois luxury that was decadent was nearly done in when dog fanciers from Hong Kong and Macao (where luxuries, decadence, and bourgeois tastes are treasured characteristics) decided to see if there were any shar-pei left. A gentleman from Hong Kong named Matgo Law joined forces with a Mr. Chung Ching Ming, and the breed was pulled back from the edge of the pit, apparently at the last moment.

The shar-pei has had good press. Its scarcity, its bizarre appearance, and its romantic history may actually carry it forward toward some small degree of popularity. It does not seem to be the kind of dog that will make the top-ten list, but one cannot account for changing tastes and the need of people to have something different.

I have known only three examples of shar-pei. My first impression was neutral. I tend to like any dog that doesn't dismember me, and these few were certainly pleasant enough. I am partial to wrinkles in my dogs (bulldog and bloodhound, to name two favorite Caras household breeds), and I do understand what may seem to be unconventional views of beauty. I hope the shar-pei flourishes, because inside that strange exterior beats the heart of a real dog, and a lot of people seem to be attracted to it. That should be enough for anyone.

In Israel there is a popular dog that is beginning to attract attention here as well. The canaan dog is being bred by a number of kennels in California, and this forty-to-forty-five-pound general-purpose dog may soon start making canine news. To its credit it has served in recent conflicts as a general-utility dog in the Israeli army. It can be used as a guide for the blind and is a natural watchdog. It has a medium coat and a curled tail and is well proportioned. It is a very doggy-looking dog and is characteristically strongly attached to its human family. Almost any color combination is allowed. Its following here is intense if not yet large.

The love of dogs in Israel is an interesting phenomenon and does not generally arise from the *sabra* or indigenous Jewish element. For thousands of years, Jews in the region have led a difficult existence beset by dangers we on the outside cannot imagine. It has been war, nothing less than that, simply to stay alive. Then along came the rather more culturally sophisticated European Jews and with them the love of luxuries like pet dogs and cats. The so-called black Jews from Arab countries have had some difficulty understanding their new compatriots' love of the companion animal—just another mouth to feed in the Middle East. But dogs have caught on, and that somewhat nondescript little canaan dog has assumed a special place, because it is of local origin—it is a *sabra*.

It is not unusual to argue the dog issue for hours. It can assume disproportionate dimensions. A few years ago I traveled with my son and two friends from just about one end of the Sinai Peninsula to the other. One of our companions was Major General Avraham Yoffe, the George S. Patton of the Israeli army, its greatest tank commander. Yoffe's troops took Sharm el Sheik in the south and then drove north to the Suez Canal. He is now retired from the army and is the head of the Nature Reserve Authority. He is Israel's greatest bird-watcher and has done more than any other single man to create the national wildlife refuges in his country, more per square mile than any nation on earth. For some strange reason General Yoffe thinks dogs are idiotic, and for the entire trip, across desert flats, through high mountain passes, through battlefields littered with crashed warplanes and burned-out tanks, we drove, argued, pouted, shouted, and fought. I don't know how we survived, since we were carrying two pistols and two submachine guns. I had fleeting fantasies about our eventually squaring off behind a sand dune and fighting it out. Avraham, a dear friend, has the Israeli national characteristic of never letting anything go once it is clamped between his teeth. He kept up his snide antidog comments and I kept knee-jerking in response when I should have been ignoring him. He was, after all, acting just like a terrier.

There are a lot of people like General Yoffe in Israel who feel that way about dogs, reflecting inadvertently, perhaps, the Arabic prejudice that is even more profound. The Israelis talk about dogs as a waste of resources by the effete while the Arabs torture or kill them. Still, there is a growing circle of real dog lovers in Israel based on habits imported with European immigrants. The dogs will win. By all indications, the Arabs unfortunately will continue to hate dogs. In the meantime, the canaan dog will have made it here and be a very popular breed. All of this will take no more than fifteen years. By that time the Israelis in general will be very boastful of *their* dog and how well it has been received around the world.

The massive, powerful neapolitan mastiff is seen occasionally in this country. Weights run as high as 150 pounds, and males may stand to twenty-eight inches or more. It is undoubtedly a descendant of the Tibetan mastiff, but there knowledge stops and theory starts. One story has the neapolitan mastiff reaching Italy on Phoenician ships in extremely ancient times. That would certainly have been possible. The Phoenicians were running around the Mediterranean with all kinds of trade goods. They may even have been using mastiffs as guards when their ships were tied up in port. Then there is the theory that has the neapolitan a Greek development that eventually reached Rome. It is said to have been one of the fighting dogs of the Roman arenas. Alexander is said to have admired them in Greece. They have been known in Campania since ancient times. It will never be sorted out, but this variation on the Tibetan-mastiff theme is known in this country to just enough people to suggest that it may one day be one of us, bringing all of its ancient mystery and history with it. One has the distinct impression when looking at the neapolitan mastiff that one should be very pleasant to its owner. This is a guard dog and probably has enough strength in its jaws to bend an I-beam or carry a railroad tie up a flight of stairs. It is loyal, stubborn, and territorial. It is a dog for dog fanciers to watch and people of ill will to watch out for.

We have alluded to the explosive subject of law-and-order and dogs several times, and it is a subject that warrants a moment's digression. We assume, on reasonable grounds I think, that dogs have been bred for guard or watch duty from very early in their domestic career. Whether it was protecting cattle or kids, sheep or the shepherd himself, they have been bred to protect, to possess, and to jealously watch over that which is theirs. Those factors have had a great deal to do with canine styling. The whole mastiff line undoubtedly arose to protect people and property. Crime has probably had as much to do with shaping today's dogs as any other single factor.

In recent years, in the United States and most large European cities as well, there has been a marked upswing in violent crime accompanied by a new leniency in dealing with it. Anyone who has not watched crime statistics climb and court rulings soften has been living in a paper bag on a distant planet. There is an inevitable vigilante mentality that arises in times like these, and since the Colt-on-the-hip kind of thing is out except in some parts of the Third World, notably Latin America, the dog has been the weapon of choice. As crime has risen and punishment has fallen, dogs have grown in size. It is not difficult to graph. Virtually any dog that offers intimidation, territoriality, and deterrence has a chance to make it into the big time. The doberman pinscher has gone from way down in the popularity lists to the number-two spot since the general demise of capital punishment, while the German shepherd has stayed up in fourth place. In a very few years the St. Bernard went from twenty-ninth place in popularity to ninth.

Until we get Genghis Khan in the judge's seat we can reasonably expect the larger dogs, the potentially more protective breeds, to continue their climb. It is not a good trend. Purposefully getting a potentially aggressive dog that could be hard to manage for the reasons suggested cannot help but lead to accidents. Certainly that is true if the dogs have been attack-trained. Accidents with large dogs can be fatal, and restrictive legislation is bound to follow. We don't all pack guns; should we all pack "killer dogs"?

There is an alternative to the protection dog, and that is strict obedience training. I would support any legislation that made basic obedience certification a legal requirement for owning and licensing any dog at all, certainly any dog weighing over twenty-five pounds. It is hard to argue the fact that people just don't get raped and mugged while walking a doberman or a shepherd or a rottweiler. It would be comforting, though, to know that all of those dogs were under perfect control. All are extremely intelligent as well as extremely loyal, and misbehavior on their part is the owner's fault entirely. The neapolitan mastiff fits into this discussion because, like the mastiff we know somewhat better and its derivative the bullmastiff, this giant Italian has been bred for millennia and is bred today to watch over the family and its possessions. Its mere presence is usually enough to suggest that thieves and worse move along and mind their own business. A dog like that has fertile ground to grow in the United States today.

In earlier discussion of the working dogs I spoke of the relatively new Japanese import the akita. It is rapidly gaining in popularity in this country because of the many fine qualities the Japanese built into the breed. The Japanese tend to be meticulous about everything they do from carp and goldfish breeding to gardening, cooking, and dog breeding. Everything is raised to the level of an art, and indeed that holds true for the akita. In Japan one encounters other breeds as well, generally on a lead and always well groomed. There are also street dogs, pariah dogs, and in remote villages undoubtedly random-breds.

If one consults the literature, almost inevitably there is a sentence starting, "There are five kinds of dogs in Japan . . ." and then it goes on to list five that are quite different from those suggested by the last authority consulted. In fact, Japan does have a small variety of homemade full-blooded dogs, and considering the amount of commercial exchange between the United States and Japan and the Japanese genius for the export business it is not at all unlikely that we will be seeing more of the Japanese breeds before too much longer.

The akita is the only established dog in this country that really is of Japanese origin. The Japanese chin, formerly called the Japanese spaniel, is of Chinese origin and showed up in Japan, presumably as a gift to the emperor, a relatively short time ago. It has certainly been less than a thousand years and probably much less than that.

In Japan today, and seldom if ever encountered here, is the kyushu or ochi dog. It is most commonly found on the island of Hokkaido. It is medium-sized (twenty-one inches tall) and used for hunting and guard work. It is apparently

a very old breed and is known for its stamina in mountain-
ous country. In style, coat, and ears and tail set, it is not
unlike the akita, although considerably smaller and lighter.
The nineteen-to-twenty-inch-tall hokkaidoken or ainu dog
is another tough and tenacious animal reportedly used for
bear hunting. It is said to attack an animal nearly ten times
its weight without hesitation. In 1937 the Japanese government extended official protection to the breed and gave it
its present name.

The tosa or Japanese fighting dog is mastiff-like in conformation, although it is quite a bit smaller than that breed
as we know it, seldom over ninety pounds. It probably
traces back no further than the middle of the nineteenth
century, to the Meiji era. Great dane, bulldog, bull terrier,
and possibly St. Bernard were used with local Japanese
breeds to develop the new strain. It is a breed said to be
famous for its fighting courage and its patience with human
companions. It is so like other mastiff-type dogs that it
would probably be the least likely of the Japanese breeds to
make it here.

Besides the akita, a fighting dog up until 1925 when the
Japanese passed a law forbidding its use in combat, there is
the popular san shu. It originated in the department of
Aichi, where kyushu from the area were crossed with chow
chows. The final touches were put on the breed in the
period just preceding World War I and the breed has
spread throughout Japan, enjoying considerable popularity
as a pet and house guard. Like all of the true Japanese
breeds, with the exception of the mastiff-like tosa, the san
shu has a curled tail. That curled tail may reflect Japanese
taste, but it also clearly establishes the northern-spitz origin
of all of these breeds. Only the tosa has been overwhelmed
by European bloodlines, with the St. Bernard and great

dane, both descendants of the Tibetan mastiff, finally determining the general outline of the animal.

The Japanese breeds have been outlined in some detail here because there is a strong likelihood that some of them will be making their way here just as the akita has. We can only hope that breeders here will be as meticulous as their Japanese counterparts and the akita will retain the qualities the GI's admired so much when they first saw the animal during the World War II occupation. If other breeds are in fact to follow it would be nice to think that the extremely high sense of aesthetics that filters down through everything the Japanese are serious about will infect enthusiasts here.

There is not a single canine design seen today in the United States that is not repeated time and time again in countries all around the world. Fewer than half the known breeds are even seen in this country, much less shown. The basic themes, though, perhaps reflecting local taste in small details, hold true all over the world. As one travels it is impossible not to be struck by almost-familiar dogs one encounters. You can see the spitz or the foxhound or the terrier or the mastiff showing through, all with variations on the basic themes.

Reflecting once again on the travels of dogs as they achieved their present diversity, you have to wonder how it was possible. Take that tosa mastiff-like dog in Japan. We know that dogs originated in the Middle East, or at least we think we know that. Somewhere between eight and twelve thousand years later they showed up in Idaho, this long before we can trace the journeys of or even accurately identify human travelers to the western hemisphere. Then a mastiff-like monster appears in Tibet. We are still thousands of years back in history. Then the mastiff strain from

Tibet appears in Greece and Rome and spreads up through all of Europe. Its descendants are then back in Japan being crossed with local spitz-stock breeds.

None of that would be surprising, *if it happened today.* You put a dog in a crate, you put the crate on a 747, and in a matter of hours the dog is anywhere in the world where the landing strips are long enough to handle the aircraft. But in the era when the original domestic dog strains were moving back and forth across the world, travel was by caravan. A journey from Egypt to Tibet took years. Children were born, grew up, and died on a single journey. The death rate among the human participants on these epic journeys was high; disease, weather, avalanche, bandits, war, poor navigation, deserts, impassable mountains, swollen rivers, all must have taken a horrendous toll on man, horse, camel, and dog. However many dogs got through, it must have been a very tiny number compared with the numbers that started out. Given the life span of a dog, often far less than ten years for the mastiff-like dogs, a dog that started out may have never gotten to its master's destination. Its offspring probably finished the trip for it. There was no protection against disease for man or dog, and certainly diseases like distemper, rabies, and other viral strains we may not even know today must have infected the travelers, since the diseases could come to the travelers from local dogs along the way as well as from wildlife. On those journeys the traveling dogs surely bred at every opportunity with animals in the villages they encountered. There were pariah dogs, certainly, in every marketplace, and the traveling bitches, too, must have been infused with local genes at oases and river fords. Caravans coming from different parts of Europe and Asia met and often overwintered together. Breeding must have been constant.

That is all history, and we will never untangle it. We will wonder about it as long as we have dogs. I often think about it when I look at our dogs. *What stories could you tell? How much human history must there be in you? Where have you been, and isn't it wonderful that you simply don't care where you're going? Being a mirror to history and keeping your counsel is surely a very sophisticated way to be.*

7
The Dog Show: Heaven Help Us

The dog show. A fete as crazed as a block party in Iran, a celebration of the dog, of man, and of sporting ambition, a sporting event as genteel on the surface as the U.S. Open but as heavy underneath as a hockey game. All of that and more. The first recorded event of this kind took place in 1859 in Newcastle-on-Tyne. There were six judges pinching and prodding sixty pointers and setters. The next year, 1860, there was a show in Birmingham as well. The idea stuck and has never come unstuck. The fact that prickly people can make it a little sticky at times has done nothing to dull the sport's luster. It was and is a fine idea even if it does appear at times to have been invented by a sardonic prankster.

If animals bring out both the best and the worst in people, and it is my premise that they do, the dog show magnifies all that several score times. The better get better and the worse get incredibly worse. A dog show is a cross between an office picnic, a bloodless bullfight, root-canal work, a Miss America pageant, and a tax audit by an IRS person who is jealous of you, as they all are. You get most of your flat tires of the year going to dog shows, take most of your wrong turns and get your most iridescent sunburns and best soakings, all the while wondering not only what everyone else around you is doing, but what you are doing yourself, perhaps even *to* yourself.

Dog shows have a purpose. The idea, ostensibly, is to isolate, through competition and elimination, those dogs and bitches that are most worthy of not being in isolation come breeding time. The idea is to make a reputation for a dog or bitch (in this one chapter I will get properly technical: "dog," like "drake," means "male," and "bitch," like "duck," means "female," and don't ask me—I don't know —why they are not called dog and bitch shows) so that everyone will be mad to have its young. That means your male dog will be called upon to play stud and your bitch can acquire the services of the best dogs, all of which will cost you money and time and bring you absolutely immense pleasure and enduring poverty. If you allow yourself to get the least bit serious about showing dogs, you are lost. It is not just a sport, it is a form of cannibalism. It eats people, their means and manners, and can make them quite mad. Showing dogs is also a real sport and a family project. It has somehow acquired an aura of elitism that is no longer justified. A dog show today, in fact, is about as elite as H. & R. Block. Anyone can play. If the sport does make you crazy it is you, not it, who are at fault. You are also, in all likelihood, insufferable at a prizefight, murder at a hockey game, and a positive yahoo at a state fair. A dog show is where you let yourself go. So do dogs.

There are people who make a great deal of money at dog shows—they are professionals, handlers, groomers, people who work harder than any people I know—and others who not only make nothing but spend a great deal. It is not at all clear who enjoys the game more. It is even less clear that in the long run it matters. You will forever remember the day that your lovely Ch. Fig Newton Phydeaux won the group. You will soon forget what it cost. You can always sell your grandfather's watch. You cannot often know true glory intimately.

How does it work? Quite well, considering the absolute insanity that seems to be in control. It really does work. To understand how requires that you relax and drop your guard. Differentiate between stupid and ignorant and acknowledge, if necessary, the latter.

As I said earlier, all dogs being shown are divided into seven groups. At this point we are talking about conformation shows, not field trials, not trailing trials, and not obedience trials. They may or may not occur in conjunction with a conformation show, but it would certainly muddle things up if I tried to work them in here. I will strive for minimum muddle and stick to conformation.

There are two basic forms of conformation shows, benched and unbenched. In the unbenched show, people come onto the show grounds or into the building with their dogs in time to show them. If they have no reason to stay after they have done so, they are free to leave. Many do hang around to gossip and watch the action and judge the judges. There never has been a dog show where the dogs get as thorough a going-over as the judges do. In a benched show the exhibitors must be on site by a certain time and can leave no earlier than a certain time. Ten in the morning to nine in the evening would be typical. Benched shows are, by and large, more elegant than unbenched shows, but tend to be harder on dogs and people alike. They have one tremendous advantage: they attract crowds who can come at any time during the posted hours and see all the dogs and meet the breeders and even some of the celebrated handlers. Benched shows are more festive. People even wear gowns and tuxedos to some. They can get very messy by the end of the day.

Before getting down to how shows actually work, I must point out another distinction. There are point shows and match shows. Match shows are fun contests, sort of like a 4-H meeting in Guccis, where no championship points are earned and judging is almost inevitably on a much lower plane. (I know that to be true, because I have judged match shows.) People with puppies may decide to give their novices experience at a few match shows before going on to point shows. People with dogs that are clearly not destined to set the world of purebred dogs atitter may go to match shows for the fun of it and to let their children participate and have at least a chance of getting a ribbon or perhaps even a trophy. Match shows also give prospective judges an opportunity to try their eye out on breeds for which they are not yet licensed in point shows. A point show is simply a full-blown show where a dog or bitch has a chance to earn points toward its championship.

Now, let us say we have a licensed show with licensed judges all approved by the AKC with AKC representatives (called, of course, "reps") on the grounds. The sponsoring dog club is a member club of the AKC, and a supervising company that does nothing but supervise dog shows under contract has set up the tents and laid out the rings, having mailed entry forms well in advance to known dog-show participants. The catalog is printed and on sale for $2, the local volunteer fire department has set up a hotdog stand with rotund, good-natured fellows in aprons with absurd sayings on them aiding the ladies' auxiliary behind oilcloth-covered collapsible tables with tubs and tubes of mustard teetering amid vast boxes of horrendously sweet frosted doughnuts. Local police are sweating themselves into a blind rage over people double-parking to unload their cockers, crates, kids, and camp chairs, the local humane group has a contribution table with photographs of dogs available for adoption posted, the vendors who work the shows have positioned display racks of chains, collars, leads, and stainless-steel food dishes and coat glossers—all is in order and in place. You have to be careful where you step, the loudspeakers are calling the clean-up crew to ring six and the photographer to ring nine. How does it work? What really is going on besides bedlam?

Trust me. It really can be understood if you relax and let it happen to you. Accept the fact that you are quite mad, or at least masochistic, and you, too, can show your dog.

Every dog and bitch on the show grounds (inside or out; out is better if the weather is good) is either already a champion or is trying to become one. That distinction is absolute. Everything that follows below stems from that fact.

Dogs and bitches that are not yet champions are referred to as class dogs or bitches. They are in the classes, and they are separated by breed and by sex. There are any number of classes, and by no means will one show have all classes for all breeds for both sexes. As a matter of fact, it is extremely rare for a show to have even all the recognized breeds present. Some, like the classic Westminster Kennel Club Dog Show in Madison Square Garden in New York City, may have close to all the breeds and varieties, but a full house is a rare occurrence.

Now, the classes. There are Puppy Class—Dogs and Puppy Class—Bitches. Those are animals over six months of age, but under one year of age. There may be a further breakdown of six to nine months and nine to twelve months, but not generally. There is an Open Dog Class and an Open Bitch Class. Anyone can put an entry in one of those classes as long as the dog or bitch is six months old or older. You don't have to go into the Puppy Class if you think your entry is good enough to compete with older animals. There is American Bred, Bred by Exhibitor, and any number of other classes normally reserved for dogs that have not achieved championship status. While the classes are in progress, the champions entered for competition that day (they are called "specials") are held in reserve. If it is an unbenched show they may not even be on the grounds until the classes for their respective breeds are just about over.

Remember, at this point, each breed is judged separately and each sex as well. All you will see in the ring at one time are animals of the same sex and the same breed. It is most important to keep this in mind as these separations are soon over.

Each class has its winner, or at least it usually does. The judge is not required to award any ribbons if he or she thinks the animals present in the class are below acceptable standards. In most cases, however, a winner is picked in each class, then second- and third-place ribbons are awarded. It is the holder of the blue ribbon, however, who then moves forward. Second- and third-place winners try to look pleased and variously embrace or take the hand of the blue-ribbon handler of the event. Joy, in fact, may not be the true emotion of the nonbest. Actually most participants are awfully good sports.

After all the classes for a breed and a sex are over, the

winners of each class are called back and are judged against each other. They are still separated by sex. The best of the blue-ribbon dogs and the best of the blue-ribbon bitches are singled out and designated Winner's Dog and, not at all surprisingly, Winner's Bitch. Now they alone of all the class dogs, the not-yet-champions, must be watched. Everybody else is sent packing.

Those two animals, Winner's Dog and Winner's Bitch, get points toward their championship. The number of points varies from show to show depending on two things: the number of animals of that breed of each sex entered that day and the part of the country where the show is staged. There is a chart that indicates how many points a ten-dog or ten-bitch entry, or a twenty- or thirty-animal entry, is worth in each region. That can vary tremendously. To win three points in, let us say, Massachusetts you would have to have thirty-one doberman pinscher dogs or thirty-four bitches, but only four borzoi dogs or five borzoi bitches. If three, four, or five points can be won for a breed, the show is called a major for that breed. I will come back to points and majors in a moment.

Winner's Dog and Winner's Bitch are now called back into the ring, along with all the champions in that breed registered to show that day. The judge picks Best-of-Breed, affectionately referred to in the dog world as BOB. No champion earns points, for, as we will see in a moment, they don't need them. The BOB is now set aside, and I will come to *that* in a moment. (I have to keep all this flowing forward, as it does in a show.) At the same time the judge is picking BOB he or she is also picking Best-of-Winners and Best-of-Opposite. Stay calm. This is no time to buckle under to hysteria. It is really quite simple.

Best-of-Winners is the choice between Winner's Dog and

Winner's Bitch. Now, if the chart shows that the show offers
more points to bitches than to dogs in that breed because
of the numbers entered in the show and the part of the
country where the show is held (remember that?) and the
dog or male is chosen Best-of-Winners, the dog gets the
differential in points added to his score without taking any
away from the bitch. We will run that by once more. Let us
say it is a three-point show for bitches (because there are
more bitches than dogs in the show) and a two-point show
for dogs. Winner's Dog, then, has gotten two points and
Winner's Bitch has gotten three. Then, in the last go-
around, the judge decides the male is the better of the two.
Then both animals get three points. The dog has gained by
beating the bitch, but the bitch hasn't lost. I understood all
of this perfectly clearly after only ten years of going to dog
shows. But, and this is most important when it comes to
dog-show demeanor, I always pretended I understood. You
are admired for acting as if you know something, not necessarily for knowing something. It is that way in all sports,
including politics. Only dog shows are much classier than
politics.

I touched on Best-of-Opposite above. That is just a nice
ribbon and doesn't get anyone any extra points. It simply
means that if a male is chosen BOB (remember, Best-of-
Breed), a bitch is chosen as the best entry of the opposite
sex. Naturally, the reverse is true. Chauvinism is often dis-
played. Some judges just naturally prefer dogs over bitches,
and hence the old saying, " 'Tis better to have a doggy-
looking bitch than a bitchy-looking dog." (Another saying
I always liked, usually heard after one cranky female canine
has lunged at another: "They don't call them bitches for
nothing.")

So, then, we now have all the classes over, all the nonwinners eliminated. We have the best of the blue-ribbon class dogs selected and the blue-ribbon class bitches chosen, and they have gone up against each other at the same time the specials or champions of record are in the ring. The Best-of-Winners has been chosen, the points for the two top class dogs (a dog and a bitch) have been straightened out, and the one animal, BOB, that will go on that day to represent the entire breed has been singled out. Ribbons and nasty little silver-plated nut dishes or inexpensive but crystal-looking glasses with dogs badly engraved on them have been handed out. What do the points mean?

A champion becomes a champion by earning points in the way outlined above. To be a champion (a special), to have a Ch. in front of your name, you have to have achieved two things. You have to have won fifteen points in recognized shows, and you have to have won two major shows under two different judges. You will recall that a major is a show that awards three or more points according to that old chart. Very often a competitor will win one major and then go on winning at show after show trying to get a second major. By the time that animal finally wins its second three-point show or better, it may have accumulated more than fifteen points. That doesn't matter—it still must have that second major, and that is far more difficult for some breeds than others.

The easiest dog to finish—that is, show until it becomes a champion—is a dog of low but not impossibly low popularity. A doberman pinscher, for instance, is murder to finish because you have so many of them. When you have eighty or ninety dobermans in a show, you have to have some kind of a great beast to win over all of them. On the other hand, if you have a field spaniel or an American water spaniel you may have to travel to the moon and back to find a major show to win, and to another planet to find two of them, there are so few of those animals in the country. Our breed, the bloodhound, regularly sits in the fifties in popularity. There are plenty of majors, because so few specimens are required to constitute a major, yet there are seldom so many to compete with that you have trouble winning with a good animal. If a breed stands between thirtieth and sixtieth in popularity in this country it is among the easiest to finish. Of course, there are specialties (which have nothing to do with specials).

A specialty show is a show very often staged in conjunction with a regular show where a breed club decides to make a huge event out of it and dogs of that breed come from all over to compete. There are regional specialties and national specialties. Let us say the Mid-Atlantic Bloodhound Club has its regional specialty every April in Delaware, which it does. You are likely to find between seventy and ninety bloodhounds entered instead of the usual five or ten at regular dog shows.

Winning at a specialty is a big thing, and there are all kinds of extra classes, things like Puppy Sweepstakes, Brood Bitch, Veteran's Class, Braces—it is when the enthusiasts for a given breed really have a time getting together and hissing about each other's dogs. Actually, there is enormous camaraderie and a great deal of shared joy. Old friends with two and four legs are encountered; there are picnics and dinners and guest speakers and all kinds of special trophies. People run around loaded with plated gee-gaws looking as if they have just won the company bowling league's Person-of-the-Year award. Enthusiasts try to finish their dogs at a specialty, or retire their favorite at a specialty. It is very festive, a very nice affair, and it always rains in Delaware at the bloodhound specialty, or fries all present. Indifference to weather is an absolute necessity for people who show dogs.

We still have that BOB on the shelf from a few paragraphs back. Before going on to the next-highest level, let us speak of manners. There are certain things you do and do not do at dog shows or in connection with them.

First, if you have entered a dog or a bitch and a show has been designated a major because of the numbers, you try never to withdraw your entry or fail to show if that will reduce the numbers and "break the major." People may have been waiting a long time for a major so they could at least get a crack at finishing their friend, getting it its championship, and if you withdraw without very good reason and drop the entry below the major-show minimum, you are generally considered something of a fink. People will talk about you even more than they do now.

You do not stand around ringside commenting on the entries. That is terrible, the worst kind of bad manners. Besides, the person standing next to you who is nine feet tall may be the owner's brother and may have been in an institution for aggravated assault on a gorilla. Think what you want; don't say it.

Never approach a judge before the judging begins. Truly, never. That is considered about as gauche as you can get and will only embarrass the judge and get you nowhere. Hanky-panky is not encouraged at dog shows. It is a straight game, so play it straight. Those that don't may win an extra point one day, but become outcasts in the process. They are quickly known to everyone for what they are, poor sportspersons and dog hustlers.

It is legitimate to approach a judge after *all* the judging is over and ask for his or her opinion of your animal, or even ask what was better about the animal that was put up over your entry. You will generally get a useful critique unless you make the question a challenge or whine it at the judge. The judge is interested in your breed or else he or she would never have gotten enough experience with it to be licensed by the AKC to judge it. You can, if you are a lady or gentleman about it, capitalize on the judge's expertise. But *never* before the judging, or you will be the one critiqued, not your dog.

There are lots of other little things about dog shows. Never drop a lighted cigarette on the ground. A dog can step on it, and then it will limp, and if it is limping for any reason the judge is obligated to dismiss it from the ring as unsound. Don't make distracting sounds or gestures at ringside. Don't be a clown. Poopie pillows on ringside seats are not considered funny. Don't wave at the judge even if she is your mother. Don't ever, under any conditions, allow your dog or bitch off its leash. Keep it in close and don't let it tangle with other dogs. Dogfights are surprisingly rare at dog shows because good sportspersons keep their charges under control. Don't let leashes cross or become entangled, for the same reason; there will be a fight. If your dog does not enjoy people it does not know, watch it, and warn people who stop to ask what breed your dog represents. And conversely, don't go running around hugging strange dogs. That is silly and dangerous. Dog bites occur at dog shows, but far, far less often than you might expect. Don't bring extra dogs to dog shows; most shows restrict that practice. Don't bring an animal that hasn't had all of its shots. Don't bring a sick animal. All common sense. Do unto others as you would have others do unto your dog.

A dog show is where you have a good time. It is fun. It

is an outing, but for some people it is serious business. Professional breeders, handlers, and judges earn a living at dog shows; some of them take competition far more seriously than others. Have your picnic, visit with friends, admire all the lovely dogs, compete at whatever level of intensity satisfies your needs, cheer when it is appropriate, applaud politely when cheering is overdoing it, but allow other people to participate at their own level of need. Share and be nice. That is what makes a dog show a happy event. Believe it or not, in time that becomes more important than getting another ribbon or perforated nut dish that will leak salt onto your coffee table anyway. Be British about it. Play the game true and well. Winning isn't everything, just almost everything.

Now, on with the judging. At the end of the day, or toward the end of the day, the seven groups are judged. Now every BOB, one from each breed, enters a big ring with all of the other BOBs *from its own group*. All the Hound Best-of-Breeds are in together, all the Sporting BOBs, and on down the list. A group judge, usually a very experienced person, picks Best-in-Group. There are also second-, third-, and fourth-place winners, and getting a *group placement* at any level is considered good going. A Group I, or taking the group, is a happening. It is heady stuff. That makes your entry a group dog or a group bitch and means it has even greater potential than just being a champion. A point about BOBs. They need not be champions. Occasionally but not terribly often, judges will pick a class dog or bitch, Winner's Dog or Winner's Bitch, to go up over the champions in the ring during BOB judging. We had that happen with a bloodhound only six months old. Yankee won his Puppy Class, then went in, we hoped, to get Winner's Dog. He did and then went on, we hoped even more, to get Best-of-Winners. He did that too, but simultaneously got Best-of-Breed. He was looked at carefully by the group judge, but did not place in the group. Still, it was an exciting day in Gorham, Maine.

Now, confusion. The first-time showgoer stands ringside during group judging and sees, in the hound group, for instance, a bloodhound, an afghan, a dachshund, a beagle, a borzoi, and a Norwegian elkhound along with all of the other hound breeds. "How, in heaven's name, does a judge evaluate those diverse animals against each other?" Legitimate question. The judge doesn't. The animals are not being judged against each other at all, but each against its own standard. A perfect dog of any breed is worth a hundred points. The judge is trying to determine which animal in the group most nearly approaches perfection. That animal is the group winner. It is somewhat subjective, but, then, what besides nuclear physics isn't?

For each breed there is a published standard that describes what each part of the animal should look like. And the various parts are more important in some breeds than in others, the emphasis on coat, for instance, varying considerably. Here, for comparison, are the point values of a few sample breeds. This does not describe, as the standards do, what these parts are supposed to look like (the judge knows), just what they are worth and how the judge rates the entries in the group competition:

RHODESIAN RIDGEBACK		GREAT DANE	
Ridge	20	1. General conformation	
Head	15	a. General appearance	10
Neck and shoulders	10	b. Color and markings	8

Body, back, chest, loins	10	c. Size	5
Legs and feet	15	d. Condition of coat	4
Coat	5	e. Substance	3 30
Tail	5	2. Movement	
Size, symmetry, general appearance	20	a. Gait	10
	100	b. Rear end (croup, legs, paws)	10
		c. Front end (shoulders, legs, paws)	8 28
		3. Head	
		a. Head conformation	12
		b. Teeth	4
		c. Eyes (nose and ears)	4 20
		4. Torso	
		a. Neck	6
		b. Loin and back	6
		c. Chest	4
		d. Ribs and brisket	4 20
		5. Tail	2 2
			100

GREAT PYRENEES

Head	
Shape of skull	5
Ears	5
Eyes	5
Muzzle	5
Teeth	5 25
General conformation	
Neck	5
Chest	5

SCOTTISH TERRIER

Skull	5
Muzzle	5
Eyes	5
Ears	10
Neck	5
Chest	5
Body	15
Legs and feet	10
Tail	2½

GREAT PYRENEES

Back	5	
Loins	5	
Feet	5	25
Coat	10	10
Size and soundness	25	25
Expression and general appearance	15	15
		100

SCOTTISH TERRIER

Coat	15
Size	10
Color	2½
General appearance	10
	100

Clearly, the emphasis shifts around. One dog may be critical on bite (the way the upper and lower teeth meet), and in other breeds that is not checked or at least the standards don't call for it as a rating point in judging. Not all breeds have actual numerical values published like those above, but the judge is supposed to know what to look for and how close to a perfect specimen what stands before him is. The group dogs are judged against their own standards and not against each other.

One little bit of action in the ring seems to confuse and embarrass newcomers to the game. In the case of male dogs only, the judge makes a quick little darting movement with his hand under the dog's rear end. He, or she, God bless her, is checking to be certain that both of the dog's testicles have descended. If one has failed to descend the dog is commonly referred to as a monorchid (*orchis* being the Greek word for "testicle") and it is disqualified. You have to have two orchids to be a champion or, of course, none. Some years ago a family had a perfectly splendid male dog that unfortunately turned out to be a monorchid. They were driven to distraction and eventually to dishonesty by their disappointment. They found an unscrupulous veterinarian who agreed to place a small silicon ball in the empty pocket of the scrotum. After the surgery had healed they entered their dog in a show and the judge did his quick feel-and-check. Then he did it again. He looked at the handler who had been hired to show the dog, and who happened to be a top person in the field, with a confused expression. "Three?" the judge asked. It seems the jostling and the excitement of coming to his first show had so stimulated the poor beast that his recalcitrant testicle had dropped into place. The dog was disqualified and the mortified handler, who knew nothing of the illegal testicular machinations of his client, was enraged (at the owner, not the judge). Ironically, monorchids can reproduce and in some countries, I am told, can be shown. But not in America. Here it is two or out you go. A little macho, perhaps. (I have always been confused by one thing. Judges often check the testicles of specials. Now these are dogs that have been judged in some cases scores of times. Clearly they have had two all along or they wouldn't have come so far. Where do the judges think they have gone?)

On the subject of disqualification, many breeds have a list of disqualifying points besides a short-count scrotal sac. Here are some examples of things the judge cannot allow to pass:

BASSET HOUND
Height of more than 15 inches at the highest
   point of the shoulder blades
Knuckled-over front legs
Distinctly long coat
BRUSSELS GRIFFON
Dudley or butterfly nose, white spot or blaze
   anywhere on coat

Hanging tongue
Jaw overshot
Solid-black coat in the smooth type
CARDIGAN WELSH CORGI
A distinctly long coat
Pure white
PEMBROKE WELSH CORGI
"The judge shall dismiss from the ring any
    Pembroke Welsh Corgi that is vicious or
    excessively shy."
BULL TERRIER
Blue eyes
In the case of the colored variety, "Any dog
    which is predominantly white."
FOX TERRIER
Nose white, cherry, or spotted to a
    considerable extent with either of these
    colors
Ears prick, tulip, or rose
Mouth much undershot, or much overshot

In addition to disqualifying faults, there are serious faults that may not get a dog kicked out of the ring, but will certainly interfere with its chances of making a good impression. The miniature schnauzer, the standards state, should not exhibit toyishness, raciness, or coarseness, and there are at least another dozen points that are listed as faults. (A miniature schnauzer can be disqualified for being under twelve inches tall or over fourteen inches tall or for being solid white or having white patches.) Major faults in the soft-coated wheaten terrier are overshot or undershot jaws, coat-texture deviation, or any color save wheaten. And so it goes. The judge who judges an entire group, or, as I shall

be discussing, potentially all breeds in Best-in-Show competition, really knows dogs. All of these minute details of all
breeds possibly seen in the ring must be known by heart,
and heart has a lot to do with judging no matter what anyone says. Judges have personal preferences. They see dogs
certain ways, and whereas one judge may like one style of
head in a breed another judge might like an altogether
different style. Well, perhaps "altogether" does approach
hyperbole; a different judge may have different ideas about
what the standards mean. After all, it takes nine Supreme
Court justices to interpret our Constitution.

People showing dogs quickly come to know judges' preferences and skip shows where a judge is not sympathetic to
their style of dog. That is fair sportsmanship. Why spend
the time and money to enter a dog in a show where it cannot
win? If you have a very good dog you really don't want to
be beaten too often. It is bad for a dog's reputation, not to
mention your ego.

Temperament can be very important in the judging process. It is not specified for all breeds, but it is for some. For
the bloodhound it is stated: "In temperament he is extremely affectionate, neither quarrelsome with companions
nor with other dogs. His nature is somewhat shy, and
equally sensitive to kindness or correction by his master."
Under the doberman pinscher we find the following re-
quirements: "The judge shall dismiss from the ring any shy
or vicious Doberman." Shyness is defined: "A dog shall be
judged fundamentally shy if, refusing to stand for examination, it shrinks away from the judge; if it fears an approach
from the rear; if it shies at sudden and unusual noises to a
marked degree." Viciousness, a terrible word to apply to a
dog, or to have to apply to a dog, is defined this way: "A dog
that attacks or attempts to attack either the judge or its

handler is definitely vicious. An aggressive or belligerent attitude towards other dogs shall not be deemed viciousness."

Under the rottweiler we find this disheartening statement: "Timid or stupid-appearing animals are to be positively rejected." And for the magnificent samoyed we read that specimens are expected to be "intelligent, gentle, loyal, adaptable, alert, full of action, eager to serve, friendly but conservative, not distrustful or shy, not overly aggressive, unprovoked aggressiveness to be severely penalized."

Of course, what is going on here in the standards and in the dog show itself is an effort to pick those dogs and bitches best deserving of having their reputations enhanced by win after win so their puppies will be in demand. Thus is the breed improved. Personally, I consider it a terrible lack of responsibility for a breed standard not to include standards for behavior and temperament. Dogs should be known for what they really are, and aggressiveness, shyness (which leads to biting almost as often as aggressiveness does), and other personality shortcomings should be penalized and bred out of the breed. Dogs that don't fit into social situations naturally and easily may one day cause so many restrictions to be put on dog-owning that people won't be able to do it anymore. I really do not understand how a group of fanciers, whatever their breed, can think of coat length, texture, or color as more important than whether the dogs they are producing eat children or not.

There are surprisingly few accidents at dog shows, although most judges get bitten sooner or later. Dogs can have off days just as people can, and just like the Newfoundland that nailed me in a veterinary clinic any other naturally gentle breed can turn up a tricky or waspish specimen or a good one that is not feeling up to snuff the day the judge leans over to check its inventory back aft.

Misbehavior in the ring must be evaluated against natural breed characteristics, as the doberman behavior standard indicates. A bunch of fox terriers in a ring should be very interested in eating the haunches off each other, but that should not be the case with collies. But aggression toward its own handler, other handlers, or the judge is not permitted for any breed. I once saw a judge dismiss an entire class of dogs (I don't think I will specify the breed here simply because it might be taken as an attack on the breed). There was not one dog in the ring that would stand still for examination. They all swirled around their handlers' legs like maniacs whenever the judge came near them. He waved them all out and refused to give a single ribbon. He was quite right. Who needs dogs like that to breed and produce puppies that will be going into homes?

There are very definite standards for the judge's behavior as well. Each dog in the ring is handled by a single person. It may be the owner or breeder handling his or her own dog or a professional who has been engaged. There is no question at all that a highly skilled handler can make a dog look its best. No handler can fix a faulty skeleton, but faults can be minimized and strong points accented by a good solid professional with twenty or thirty years of experience.

The handler, whoever he or she is, will be wearing an armband with a number on it. The steward assigned to the class checks off the dog by that number and informs the judge when every dog to be judged is present. The judge is then supposed to concentrate on the dogs and pick the best specimen according to standards. Of course, life is never perfect. There are some handlers who are so extremely well known, so celebrated, that they actually intimidate some judges. Not all judges are susceptible, but some are. They know the handler knows more about dogs than they do. If Jane Forsythe (now retired), or her husband Bob Forsythe (now retired), or Peter Greene, or Bill Trainor, to name just a few, appears in the ring with a dog or bitch, the judge knows that animal has to be tops, and it is possible that the sheer weight of a handler's reputation will have influence on the judge. Peter Greene, who specializes in terriers, is not going to appear in a ring at Madison Square Garden with a goat on a string. It is going to be a terrier with the potential of true stardom. The same thing can be said about any number of handlers. Many of today's top judges were originally handlers themselves. No one is going to put anything over on Ann Rogers Clarke, one of today's top judges, because she was herself probably as good a handler as the sport of dog showing has ever known. (Before Jane Forsythe married Bob Forsythe she was Jane Camp. Before Ann Rogers Clarke married judge Jim Clarke she was Ann Holme Rogers. Jane and Ann were two of the top handlers the world has ever seen. I get confused. On a television special I once referred to Ann, or Annie as she is affectionately called by everyone who knows her, as Jane Clarke. Jane Forsythe loved it, but Ann called me a terrible name the next time she saw me. There are risks at every level of dog showing.)

Setting aside the possible intimidation factor, a prominent judge judging a fine group of dogs is probably not encountering many strangers. Any number of times I have discussed the Best-in-Show judging with Best-in-Show judges (*after* the show) and been told that that judge not only knew every handler in the ring but every dog and had in fact judged every one of the dogs not once but several times. The point is, however, that the judge is not supposed to look at the program or any other reference telling who is showing what or who owns which dog. The judge, as nearly as humanly possible, is supposed to walk into the ring and start judging dogflesh. The fact that an experienced judge will know the best dogs from previous encounters and will recognize, very often, the style of certain kennels in the breeding cannot be avoided and thus cannot be faulted. There is less nonsense in dog showing than in many other sports I have known and loved. At the number-one dog show in the country, the Westminster Kennel Club Dog Show, held in February at Madison Square Garden, the Best-in-Show judge is not allowed anywhere near the Garden until the second night, when the Best-in-Show field of six dogs is ready. The judge walks in without knowing who has won the groups and therefore who will be in the ring. In walk the six dogs (including bitches, of course) and the judging commences. At that level, B-I-S at Westminster, the dogs are certain to be personally known to any judge worthy of that highest of all judging assignments.

The Best-in-Show, as you would suspect, caps the show. The seven group winners are assembled for this final event. A highly qualified judge licensed for all recognized breeds, again judging each animal against its own standard of perfection, picks the top dog of the day. In cases like Westminster, distillation over two days and two nights has brought roughly three thousand entries down to seven; less than one out of every five hundred dogs entered in the show makes it to that final competition. The dog chosen as Best-in-Show makes history and does wonders for its own breed as well as for its own reputation. The kennel that produces that superstar and the dog's handler are not harmed by the ensuing publicity, either.

The only bad effect of the whole thing is popularity. A breed that wins at top dog shows like Westminster, especially Westminster, is likely to be in demand almost immediately. Extreme notoriety is not generally very good for a breed even if it is financially a happy event for some breeders.

So there you have the pyramidal structure of the dog show. In a big show, between two and three thousand dogs are registered for judging, starting in the morning (a show may be one or two days long), and at the next to the last moment there are seven left, then one. A lot of people have worked very hard to produce superior specimens and worked very hard to train them and groom them and give them good ring manners. Money, time, love, hope, and camaraderie are all involved. Although the dogs may, at times, seem better behaved than some of the people, by and large it is a kind of nicely glorious event.

I can't really leave the dog show, not just yet, without introducing a brief discussion of snobbery. I think one of the most idiotic things I have ever seen in print is a sticker one sees on the back of vans or on station-wagon bumpers that says CAUTION: SHOW DOGS. I feel a mild but nonetheless distinct urge to ram any vehicle displaying the sticker (which is for sale at any dog show), because it says all the wrong things in exactly the right way. It suggests that if the vehicle contained anything but show dogs, such as dogs that were not show dogs, or aged nuns, or blind children, or brilliant brain surgeons, or any other category of living creature, it would be all right to be careless, to tailgate, crowd, or otherwise harass the driver of the vehicle. But *show dogs!* Certainly not! Extreme caution is required. That is not what dogs are all about.

Of course, there is snobbery involved in having successful show dogs, but not in the way that bumper sticker suggests. There is pride in ownership, pride in accomplishment, exactly the same kind of pride one would encounter at a 4-H or FFA meeting, or a philatelic club's display of rare postmarks, or at a book fair or any other place where people display their fruits of hard labor or labors of love.

But what about purebred dogs in general? Are they worth the cost of breeding and maintaining, especially when, as I will be discussing, there is a horrendous surplus of dogs in America? Why breed more dogs when there are too many already?

As I suggested earlier, purebred dogs are historical accomplishments. Tracing back, very often, thousands of years, they are extremely fragile reminders of ideas people have had and things people have done to realize concepts of perfection. A bulldog is English history representing sociological growth as man put things like bull and bear baiting behind him. The bulldog has a standard of beauty, believe it or not, and people love that look. If bulldog breeders should stop today, the bulldog, with its relatively short life span of approximately nine years, would obviously be extinct in a decade. It could be built again, because the dog species would not be extinct, but that could take at least scores of years. Every breed of dog, representing as it does its own history, the history of the time and place where it emerged, and mankind's continuing interest in it, is worth preserving. That can be done only if very careful breeders continue to breed only the best and never in haste or surplus. Wild animal species are not the only animals to be endangered. Many forms of livestock and companion breeds are also in danger of vanishing.

As long as people respect dogs and have concern for their own accomplishments, the history of their own taste and sense of style, and as long as human beings appreciate beauty, the purebred dog as a piece of genetic art will be fostered. The best way to keep it all going, to select the best, to eliminate that which does not represent intent in style and beauty, is to engage in a sport called dog shows. As for the elitists who put stickers like CAUTION: SHOW DOGS on the back of their cars and rigs, may they get what they deserve. After all, a sticker like that seems to be boasting of money (which show dogs by no means represent today as they once did), and anyone who wants to boast of being loaded, with the crime rate what it is today, is probably asking for broken windows and missing possessions. One hopes their dogs will not suffer. Dogs, show or otherwise, never use bumper stickers except to urinate on.

8

Humanity and Other Problems

It is simply not possible for me to write this book and pretend that all is well with man and dogs. Although our topic is a celebration of the joy of dogs, we should at least acknowledge areas where things can and, in fact, should certainly get better. A book about dogs really can't be responsible to its subject and not mention the problems that have arisen on parallel tracks with the advantages and pleasures of the dog and man relationship.

There can be little doubt that people were rather less sentimental about animals centuries ago than we tend to be now. As bad as things may be for animals in many parts of the world, or in the hands of many individuals, things are getting better and have been for millennia. To deny that is to ignore the Roman arena, the Chinese cookbook, the Tibetan skin trade, the bull and bear pits of seventeenth-century England, the rat pits of eighteenth-century En-

gland, and the dog pits of early-nineteenth-century England. It is true we still have clandestine dog pits in the
United States, but they are social aberrations, illegal and
nowhere an accepted norm. People today who act toward
animals as people did openly just a little over a century ago
have to skulk and hide and sneak, as befits them.

Travel in the Third World today still reveals poor treatment of animals. Around much of the Mediterranean periphery, life for animals can be trying. Of course, there are
devoted dog fanciers in Italy, Spain, southern France, and
Greece, but they are almost exceptions. In the Middle East,
animals are treated like vermin, unless they are sporting
dogs and can be bet on or are valuable beasts of burden or
food producers. In Israel there is a gentler attitude toward
all animals. Two thirds of the Israelis are of European origin, and they brought their capacity for loving dogs with
them as a cultural heritage.

In Arab countries there is a resentment directed toward
dogs that is mind-boggling. Only fine coursing hounds are
treated like living creatures, and in some places—the Mal-
dives come to mind—dogs are totally banned by law.

Some people in impoverished areas may "take it out" on
animals, although those are not poor people in the boxes
at bullfights. Perhaps, though, the tradition that fosters animal combat starts with the frustrations of the poor and
becomes so established within a culture that the upper
classes eventually follow suit. In Elizabethan England and
even much later in that same country it was not the poor
who pitted their dogs, it was wealthy merchants looking for
diversion in the marketplace and young rakes and British
scalawags. Very often titled people, people of extraordinary
means, participated. People who attend illegal dogfights

and cockfights in the United States today are by no means poverty-stricken. They are frequently heavy bettors and may carry far more cash in their jeans than you and I are likely to. Their necks may be red but their money is distinctly green.

Rabies may have something to do with ancient attitudes toward dogs persisting in some areas. In places like Turkey and North Africa, and in many parts of the tropics and subtropics particularly, rabies is no joke. Practically no one dies of that disease in the United States (no one does in England), but it is hell elsewhere and must have been absolutely incredible centuries ago. Perhaps the fact that pariah dogs are a natural reservoir for the disease (the virus is said to be enzootic, resident in the native animal population) had something to do with antidog attitudes—at least with the apparent attitude that dogs don't feel pain, or it doesn't matter if they do. A rabid dog is not usually pitied. It is the enemy of every mammal in the community, including human beings. The term "mad dog" has such horrifying connotations it isn't hard to see how the rabid dog has always been regarded with terror.

As soon as man had domestic dogs, he got wild dogs, or, more accurately, feral dogs. The word "feral" refers to anything that was once domesticated but has returned to the wild. (The word also applies to almost certainly mythological children raised by she wolves or other wild animals.) Feral dogs are now and have been throughout domestic canine history a scourge on livestock. Goats and sheep, particularly, seem to attract dog packs, and very often the job of the shepherding dog has been to chase away or kill not wolves, not bears, and not wild cats, but feral dogs very much like themselves in appearance.

Ask any farmer today about his experiences with stock-killing dogs and you will get a lecture, not an answer. Dogs are supposed to be under our control, and when we fail in that task we add to the ancient habit of dog hating, by providing fuel for that hate. The answer is simple. We should produce no more dogs than there are good homes, and then we should keep our dogs at home.

The almost universal dread of the wolf (old-timers in northern Sweden won't even say the word "wolf" for fear of summoning up a curse; they refer only to the "old gray one") must have been transferred in some degree to the wolf's close kin and descendant, the domestic dog. Werewolves must have reflected on dogs. And the "hounds of hell," the Hound of the Baskervilles, and other assorted villains are not missing from our literature. Ferocious canines guarded mythological caves full of gold and precious stones, and the cur-dog was an element of the best cursing heard for centuries. Witness Shakespeare, who certainly reflected the mood at the end of the sixteenth century in England:

> A pox o' your throat, you bawling,
> blasphemous, incharitable dog!
> —*The Tempest,* I, i

> And even for that do I love you the more.
> I am your spaniel; and, Demetrius,
> The more you beat me, I will fawn on you:
> Use me as your spaniel, spurn me, strike me,
> Neglect me, lose me; only give me leave,
> Unworthy as I am, to follow you.
> What worser place can I beg in your love,—

And yet a place of high respect with me,—
Than to be used as you use your dog?
                    —*A Midsummer Night's Dream,* II, i

Pish for thee, Iceland dog! thou prick-ear'd
cur of Iceland!
                    —*Henry V,* II, i

Who ever saw the like? what men have I!
Dogs! cowards! dastards! I would ne'er have fled,
But that they left me 'midst my enemies.
                    —*1 Henry VI,* I, ii

And so it goes, play after play, scene after scene, character after character. The dog is to be beaten, to be called a dog is to be roundly cursed, and if Shakespeare did nothing else he reflected brilliantly his time, its manners, its beliefs, and its frame of mind. If Shakespeare uses the word "dog" as a curse it was indeed a foul curse in his time.

It is interesting, however, that the coin was often flipped. Greyhounds were spoken of by Shakespeare's characters almost in a tone of awe. Even spaniels, beagles, and other field dogs were admired in his language, or the language of the people he cast so magnificently in the mold of his period. It is a repetition, almost, of the attitude of Islam toward dogs. Fine, purebred gaming animals are revered while all other dogs are filth. You kick and curse one and invite the other into your tent. But that is the way people treated people as well. Harsh times are harsh times.

As far as Asia goes, worse ambivalence yet. The emperor's sleeve dogs have already been discussed, and so have the dogs that were raised as food. A puppy that at nine months was to be strangled for the pot certainly got less affection than the silken creature that was to sit alongside its master on the throne. Pariah dogs in Asia to this day live a life of abuse.

It may be assumed that dogs that hung around camps and settlements as pariahs, scavengers, carriers of rabies, and possibly worriers of livestock did not fare well at the beginning any more than they did in Shakespeare's time or do today in much of the Third World. It is interesting to see how the first changes came about for that, too, as man and dog locked into parallel courses.

Before going on to see how man began to reverse what was almost certainly an ancient pattern of animal abuse, I should stop and review one of the most absurd abuses of all, capital punishment.

People obsessed with their own *eternal* safety—that is, life after death—have conjured up demons and devils by the score. With eternally malign intent the devil is always looking to get at us. When we sneeze, people bless us because it was once believed that when we sneeze our souls momentarily leave our bodies. The devil is always waiting for such an opportunity. Unless someone blesses us to hold us until our soul can get back in, the devil will fill the void. Unfortunately, the devil has often been seen in the guise of animals.

The nonsense that grew out of this fear of the devil was boundless. Termites, grasshoppers, and other pests were warned that their transgressions were endangering their own safety, and when they failed to heed the warnings (which we must assume they frequently did), they were excommunicated by the church and made to suffer the church's anathema. Animals of all kinds were regularly tried for crimes, most often murder, and the proceedings were taken seriously. In some places judges refused to try naked animals in their courts; the miscreants were dressed in human clothing and represented by defense counsels who almost invariably lost their cases.

Most of this nonsense took place in the Middle Ages, although reports go back to Ancient Greece. In the 1500s, in Germany, a cock was accused of heresy because it was said to have laid an egg. Accompanied by a crowd of jeering townspeople, the poor bewildered bird was taken out of town and burned at a stake atop a high hill. Pigs, frequent child killers in the Middle Ages, were given long prison terms. Ironically, they were put in prison with human criminals and held under identical conditions and probably fed the same slop.

It really got silly when it went beyond animate life. In China, fifteen wooden idols were put on trial for murdering a man of high military rank. They were found guilty and beheaded. In 1591 Crown Prince Dimitri, son of Ivan II, was assassinated. The bell in the town of Uglich tolled, supposedly to summon up a revolution. The bell was tried and exiled to Siberia.

Dogs, of course, did not escape this travesty. In Austria a drummer's dog bit a member of the municipal council on the leg. The drummer, rather than pay damages, delivered the dog up for prosecution under the criminal code. The dog was sentenced to one year's imprisonment in a *Narrenkötterlein*, a kind of pillory or iron cage in the center of a marketplace. It was used for blasphemers, rowdies, peacebreakers in general. The dog served his one year, as far as we know, being mocked, pelted with filth, and generally treated like a human being.

In a body of Indian beliefs and procedures known as the Avesta it is clearly stated that a mad dog shall have no recourse and be "punished with the punishment of a conscious and premeditated offense by progressive mutilation, corresponding to the number of persons or beasts it has bitten, beginning with the loss of its ears, extending to the crippling of its feet and ending with the amputation of its tail." In Rome, until fairly recently, a night attack on the city by the ancient Gauls was celebrated. On the occasion some watchdogs had failed to give the alarm, but some geese did. In the festival the geese were given gifts of food and a dog was crucified.

In the oldest surviving digest of South German law, all the domestic animals in a household, including, of course, the dogs, were treated as accessories to any crime committed by the householder and given the same punishment. They were beaten as their master was beaten and burned as he was burned.

Bestiality was looked upon with particular revulsion in the Middle Ages. (It isn't exactly applauded today.) The typical court order in these cases was that man and animal be burned alive, together. In 1606, in Loens de Chartres, a man named Guillaume Gutart was found guilty of sodomy upon a bitch. He was sentenced to death by being knocked on the head and then both were burned, "reduced to ashes."

The practice of blaming animals for human sexual misconduct made its way to the New World. In New Haven in 1662, a strange fellow named Potter, then about sixty, was executed for buggery—"damnable buggery," according to Cotton Mather. His various partners were also put to death, but there is some confusion. Old Potter himself had executed one of his friends, a bitch. He had hung her. An effort to deny the court her testimony, perhaps, or a lover's spat?

The nonsense of treating animals as if they were human

criminals with the ability to understand both what they do and what the end results of their deeds might be did not escape the world's literature. In Racine's comedy *Les Plaideurs,* a dog steals a capon and is condemned to the gallows. The defense appears in court after the conviction, but before the sentencing, with the dog's puppies and pleas for mercy with the opening words *Venez, famille désolée.*

Whether it was dogs or any other animals, there was incredibly illogical double-think at work. On the one hand a dog (as per Shakespeare) was for beating, for kicking, for cursing with none of the protection accorded the meanest of human beings, yet the same animal could be dressed in human clothing, tried in human court, put to the rack in an effort to extract a confession (that was commonly done), and then put to death. This madness began in the time of ancient Greece and Rome and continued up until at least the eighteenth century. It is true that much of the fear that inspired these proceedings came from a fear of the devil. A kind of wild religious intensity was perhaps the foremost cause of the sorry proceedings. But there was more. The world sadly needed the evolution of humanity that came with what we today call the humane movement. Through most of history, we loved having the dog, perhaps, more than we loved the dog itself. But first, more of the devil.

Unidentified dogs, surely personifying the devil, have appeared throughout history. There are threads that link them and suggest that evil has a universal face. The dog as evil itself, unfortunately, has long had its day.

Black dogs, in many parts of Europe, have appeared as harbingers of doom or at least as a bit of bad news on the paw. In England there appeared to be a concentration of these apparitions in East Anglia. In Lincolnshire a dog regularly appears to people along certain country lanes. It is black, of course, table-high, with a long neck and a snipey snout. It brushes past people at night and then bounds away, usually jumping a fence or gate. It apparently is fairly benign. It scares the wits out of people, but does little if any other harm. People still alive have been accosted by it. (It is still better than street crime in the cities.)

The Anglo-Saxon word for Satan was *soucca,* and that is perhaps the origin of the name for Suffolk's devil dog, Black Shuck. Here again the dog brushes people's legs as they walk country lanes after dark. They never see it, however; they just feel it or sense it. Many people believe that to see it would be to die. People avoid certain fields, graveyards, and lanes the dog is known to frequent. (I should hope so!) In Essex and Cambridgeshire the same stories are told. If you ever see the dog you will die. There is a strong likelihood that you would die of a heart attack if you actually saw any of the imagined things that go bang, or woof, in the night.

In Norfolk the devil dog of the night is far more demonic and is quite thoroughly feared. It is as big as a calf and has a long, shaggy, and inevitably black coat; its eyes burn like coals in the night, as one might expect, and are the size of saucers. The dog has a demonic yowl to match its reputation. Some dog! It inhabits desolate marshland and open fields, but bounds across roads and footpaths as well when people approach. It has come so far forward in time that stories are told of drivers having to slam on their brakes to avoid hitting the devil dog as it bounded in front of them. When drivers are slamming on their brakes you know you are out of the Middle Ages (but not necessarily the Dark). It is interesting to note that Norfolk's version of Black Shuck doesn't leave footprints no matter how sodden the ground. Interesting that devils either appear without a body and leave footprints or appear in a heavy doglike form and leave none. No one in his right mind in Norfolk would let his eyes meet those of Black Shuck, for to do so would be to condemn oneself to death within the year. Black Shuck often pads up behind people on country roads—a favorite trick—and breathes on them. His breath is like an icy wind. People don't turn around to check him out. Not all that surprisingly, they press on seeking shelter. Inevitably there are tales of people dying of fright or at least having their hair turn white.

In the sixteenth century, Black Shuck visited a parish church in Bungay, near Norwich. The year was probably 1576 or 1577. A great storm was in progress. A black dog burst into the church and like a whirlwind raced among the parishioners, scaring them half out of their wits. It wrung the neck of several (exactly how many is not recounted) and bit another man so fiercely that he shriveled up like a piece of burned leather and was mummified on the spot. There are places in that church, which shook most terribly as the dog ran around doing the devil's work, that show where the dog touched wood and stone. To this day those charred spots smell of brimstone.

In Suffolk, in the village of Blythburgh, a black dog appeared during a storm and *raised hell* inside a church full of people. It stove in a door, killed people, and left burning paw prints that remain to this day. Outside that church is a sign saying that no dogs are allowed. Presumably that is to keep things neat in the churchyard, but locals will confide in you that it is really to assure against a reappearance of Black Shuck.

The black dog of the devil (or perhaps the devil himself in the guise of a dog) has not been limited to the British

Isles. In Treves, Germany, in A.D. 857, a dog appeared during the celebration of the mass and ran around like a wild and terrifying wind. In 1341 at Messina, Italy, a dog appeared in a church, again during services, and began desecrating holy objects while the congregation and celebrants looked on in horror. Surely rabid dogs help give rise to and sustain this tradition.

The same kinds of stories appear in many parts of the world, and perhaps all of them were as inevitable as stories of dogs that have jewels falling from their mouths, dogs that perform all kinds of incredible deeds both good and dreadful. And the treatment of dogs and other domestic animals as criminals was also inevitable. Dogs have been around so long that we would naturally treat them, or creations of the night who come in their form, as we have treated each other. People used to be hung for stealing a handkerchief. People were tortured to get them to tell the truth. Certain classes of people had no rights at all and could be used as their masters pleased. Slavery in formal attire was only part of the story of the incredible abuse of humans by humans. As we treated people, so we treated dogs and other animals. But what happened as our conscience was born? How then did we view animals?

"The Society has continued its endeavors, by unobtrusive means, to promote a general feeling of kindness toward animals. . . . There is too much evidence that indifference to their sufferings is not confined to the uncultivated classes." That from the Fourth Annual Report (1878) of the Coventry Society for the Prevention of Cruelty to Animals.

"No civilization is complete which does not include the dumb and defenceless of God's creatures within the sphere of charity and mercy. . . ." Bristol & Clifton Society (P.C.A.), Forty-Seventh Report, 1891.

In Lowell, Massachusetts, on Sunday, October 11, 1891, the Rev. George Batchelor of the First Unitarian Church dedicated his sermon to the way we should treat animals, using the rather thin biblical thread Proverbs 12:10, "A righteous man regardeth the life of his beast, but the tender mercies of the wicked are cruel." The preacher said, "Any system of morals which begins and ends with human beings, not including also the whole world of animate life, is defective."

There is no doubt that by the nineteenth century there was a groundswell of sentiment toward all animals and increasingly toward dogs, although they still trailed far behind the horse. And with sentiment comes sentimentality. In 1873 the Pennsylvania Society for the Prevention of Cruelty to Animals, one of the earliest American societies, published a book called *A Plea for the Dumb Creation*, from which these extracts are taken:

> A Man of kindness to his beast is kind, But brutal actions show a brutal mind; Remember! He who made thee, made the brute; Who gave thee speech and reason, formed him mute. The life-like anxiety with which the dog is listening for his master's footsteps, man teach man a lesson of fidelity to his "Master in heaven." It is impossible fully to estimate the value of dogs, when they are well trained, well fed, and kindly treated.

Bonaparte and the Dog

The night after the battle of Bassano, the moon rose cloudless and brilliant over the sanguinary scene. Napoleon, who seldom exhibited of spirits, in the hour of victory, rode, accompanied by his staff, over the plain

covered with the bodies of the dying and the dead, and
silent and thoughtful, seemed lost in painful revery.

It was midnight. The confusion and uproar of the
battle had passed away, and the deep silence of the
calm, starlight night, was only disturbed by the moans
of the wounded and dying. Suddenly a dog sprang
from beneath the cloak of his dead master, and rushed
to Napoleon, as if frantically imploring his aid, and
then rushed back again to the mangled corpse, licking
the blood from his face and hands, and howling most
piteously. Napoleon was deeply moved by the affect-
ing scene and turned to his officers, with his hands
pointed toward the faithful dog, and he said with evi-
dent emotion; "here, gentlemen, that dog teaches us
a lesson of humanity."

In fact, once the humane movement got rolling it was all
stops out. It was as if there had been pent up inside of the
evolving human being a desire to relate to animals, to
"brute creation" which it was almost inevitably, and pay a
debt. People, generally, were being somewhat nicer to people, too. The two phenomena seemed to go hand in hand.
Terrible aberrations were to come (the two world wars are
good examples), but there was a new direction, and it was
reflected in man's attitude toward dogs as well as in anything else.

To trace the real beginnings of the humane concern for
dogs and the legal protection they were afforded requires
a kind of time warp because they are so far out of joint in
history. In 6000 B.C. the Egyptians afforded protection to
certain dogs, or so it was inscribed on tablets. There was an
enormous schism because while a saluki, greyhound, or

other coursing hound might have a status under the law and while Anubis was a god and was venerated, pariah dogs were for kicking and killing. Quite simply, dogs weren't just dogs, but were viewed in highly stratified levels just as human society was structured. Again, dogs reflected man.

Ancient China, Babylon, and Ethiopia had laws protecting dogs, but surely those were economic steps to protect valuable property, hunting dogs or pets of noble persons. Again, pariah dogs were almost certainly without protection, but that was no less true of people who were of low birth or who had contracted leprosy. Humane laws cannot be traced back as far as ancient times. That is a dream, and so is the quote from Proverbs. It is far too thin a thread, and there was no real follow-up in the Old or New Testament. To find one sentence in the Bible and hang the premise that the Judeo-Christian religious complex *preached* kindness to animals from the beginning is too wishful even for humanitarians. Our humanity came late in the game. It was overdue.

In the Middle Ages, when dogs and everything else in sight were going to the gibbet and the stake, dogs of noblemen were protected. In fact, they had higher social status than common men. That is not really a beginning of a humane philosophy. It was nice for dogs of high birth, but not for human beings and not for all other dogs, or the rest of "brute creation." Napoleon, who had been so touched by the dog on the battlefield at Bassano (surely an apocryphal tale), issued at least one decree protecting dogs that he needed for his army. Again, the ailurophobic conqueror protected monetary and military property, not dogs, although he probably liked them.

The first truly meaningful law that recognized the rights of "dumb" animals east of the Atlantic Ocean was passed by the British Parliament in 1822. The law compelled their humane care.

The British parliamentary action of 1822 was preceded considerably by *The Body of Liberties*. They were published, all one hundred of them, in the Massachusetts Bay Colony in 1641. These were the "liberties" by which people were commanded to live. They were not exactly laws, but were described within the body of the text as "specified rights, freedoms, Immunities, Authorities and priviledges, both Civil and Ecclesiastical." Number 92 states: "No man shall exercise any Tirranny or Crueltie towards any bruite Creature which are usuallie kept for man's use." Number 93: "If any man shall have occasion to leade or drive Cattel from place to place that is far of, so that they be weary, or hungry, or fall sick, or lambe, It shall be lawful to rest or refresh them, for a competent time, in any open place that is not Corne, meadow, or enclosed for some particular use."

Here, again, there are two liberties or near-laws that command attention to what we can honestly view as humane concerns. But it was to be another 187 years before a law appeared in the New World with the same thrust. New York was the first state to put a humane law on the books, in 1828. Massachusetts followed in 1835, Connecticut in 1838, Wisconsin in the same year, and so on. The last political unit to join the parade was the Virgin Islands. Its humane law dates back only to 1921. The last state to pass humane legislation was Arizona in 1913. The fact that Arizona came to statehood late (1912) is not a mitigating factor, since Alaska also passed a humane law in 1913.

A New York gentleman by the name of Henry Bergh, popularly known as the Angel in a Top Hat (his biography, written by Zulma Steele and published by Harper & Brothers in 1942, carried that title) received a New York State charter for the American Society for the Prevention of Cruelty to Animals in 1866. By then twenty states had at least fragmentary anticruelty statutes. One point of clarification: because Bergh named his society the Amerian SPCA, people still think of it as a national organization. It was fashioned after a national organization in England, the Royal SPCA, but as chartered here it was and is a New York State organization only. There are many other SPCAs in America, but the one with "America" before its name is not linked to them. It has too little authority within its one state and none beyond its boundaries.

The New York City of Henry Bergh little resembled the city we know today. There were no more than 100,000 people within the city limits on the day Henry was born, August 29, 1813. Everybody and just about everything but the cornfields were packed below 14th Street, and life for animals was not good. The first New York State humane law wasn't to come for another fifteen years. The aristocratic, extremely well-placed and well-traveled Bergh had in him that spark that burns fiercely in a small number of people in each generation. The number is growing with each passing generation, it seems, but it has never infected a substantial percentage of the world's population. Bergh with his cane and top hat, with his spats and regal bearing, walked the streets of the slums, visited the slaughterhouses, invaded drayhorse stables, frequented the bridal paths, went anywhere and everywhere animals might be and with his commanding presence lectured, cajoled, threatened, and eventually punished anyone who would dare to be cruel to animals. He founded his ASPCA and was its dominant force for two decades. His friends included the aristocracy of

Europe and the political and intellectual elite of America.

There were cartoons about him and jokes at dinner tables up on Fifth Avenue, but the lives of dogs and all other animals have never been the same since Henry Bergh passed this way. For when the mayor of your city, the chief of police, and celebrities like Horace Greeley are your friends and when you wear custom-tailored clothes from Paris and London, when you speak with the unmistakable accent of an uptown swell, there is just so much laughing a drayman may be willing to do. At least that was true in America around the time of the Civil War. In a nation still very conscious of class, Bergh was a commanding figure.

Farther north, in Boston, Bergh had his counterpart. George Angell was born in 1823, just ten years after Bergh, in Southbridge, Massachusetts, the son of a Baptist minister. Angell was to be instrumental in founding the MSPCA, which, although it was not connected to Bergh's ASPCA in New York, had the same mission. Today, at 350 South Huntington Avenue in Boston, stands the Angell Memorial Hospital, one of the two or three most sophisticated veterinary hospitals in the world. At ten I went to work (for ten cents an hour) on the MSPCA farm in Methuen, Massachusetts, and when I was fifteen and we moved to Boston I worked at Angell Memorial, as I have already recounted. In those institutions, where I saw literally thousands of abandoned, injured, and mistreated animals mercifully destroyed, I came to understand what Bergh and Angell had been trying to tell the world. Although I was not to start a society—I had come too late for that—I was to work for many, for I felt the fire in me as well.

Neither Bergh nor Angell was known in their time as a misanthrope, and I hope that I am not one. I think I am not. Just what it is that arrests the lifelong attention of a small percentage of each generation is hard to identify. In the history of the humane movement in the United States I am a passing reporter while Bergh and Angell were cornerstones to a giant edifice; no comparison beyond that is implied. Still, the fire is there, there in my wife and in scores of other people I have known and worked with. None of us can trace its origin. When I am asked about it by sympathizers I shrug and half (but only half) jokingly suggest that it is a birth defect or perhaps a mutation in favor of our manifest destiny, humanity.

Angell was as energetic as Bergh. He traveled throughout Europe and the United States establishing liaisons that kept him not only informed but armed with allies and instant expertise. He fought the consumer battle and put an ironware company out of business in New York after learning from chemists at Harvard that its plate was poisonous. He successfully attacked a manufacturer of poisonous wallpaper. In 1877 he fought a heroic battle for the dogs of Boston.

Between 1853 and 1877 there had been only two reported deaths from rabies in Boston, and both of those diagnoses were suspect. Still, in 1877, there was a rabies scare, no reason for which has ever been found. It was, in fact, no more than a straw man. It was an excuse for a committee, and in Boston any excuse for a committee will do. A witch-hunt committee that would have made its predecessors in Salem proud was set up at City Hall, and the plan it proposed called for every unmuzzled male dog found on the streets of Boston to be shot on sight and every female dog whether she was muzzled or not. The imposing Angell, bearded and righteous, walked in on the meeting, and it wasn't long before the dog/witch hunters knew they were out of work. Angell wrote with a pen that could disembowel any committee, as he always did when he was on the campaign trail, and his words were widely circulated. The dog hunt fizzled before the first shot was fired. A bearded mountain had arisen in its path. Angell also published the first paper on humane slaughter and euthanasia, and he wrote on an imposing variety of other topics calling for the humane treatment of animals, children, laborers, and railroad engineers.

Somehow, in their day, the "do-gooders" Bergh and Angell were not looked down upon. They touched too many lives in too many ways. The jokes and the cartoons all carried an undertone of respect. In them a force was born, and it was unmistakable. There has been appalling cruelty against man and animals since their time, but the trend is in another direction. It takes a long time to change the world, but they did it; they launched changes in America, and America has never been the same since. Cruelty, at least cruelty that is tolerated, is being crowded into ever smaller pockets and has to be ever more hidden in its practice. No one will tolerate it in the streets anymore. Before Bergh and Angell they did. Among other things, Bergh and Angell, aristocrats that they were, made the humane treatment of animals in America polite, socially acceptable, even fashionable. It is no longer a subject for derision.

But back to Angell. By 1878 he was into prison reform (with considerable success), writing about communism and consumerism, campaigning in the halls of Congress for humane interstate shipment regulations for livestock, and back fighting for dogs. A law was proposed before the Massachusetts legislature that would have taxed dog owners so severely that hundreds of thousands of dogs would have had to have been destroyed or abandoned. Angell got word of it, recognized it as an extension of the rabies scare of the previous summer, and obtained a five-day adjournment of the hearing in the State House on Beacon Street. When the legislature met to discuss the tax they found the hall packed from one side to the other with dog owners, dog lovers, and dog protectionists, led by the apparently indefatigable George Angell, Esq. The law was not passed. The dog haters of Boston had once again been routed.

Between leading his endless battle against adulterous chemicals in the things people ate and used in their daily lives, his visits to schools and colleges, his appearances before legislative bodies in Washington and in state capitals across the country, and somehow between the almost endless stream of letters to editors and tracts that he turned out, Angell kept up his battle for animal welfare.

In 1882 he got a fox hunt stopped by public pressure. He was instrumental in forming Bands of Mercy to fight his battles against cruelty and by 1883 had seen the number of bands grow to over six hundred, with seventy thousand members. His work carried him to Chicago, where he repeated his Boston efforts. There seemed to be no place where he could not or would not appear. In 1873, now old enough to play the role of prophet, he wrote:

> Cruelty will become unpopular, and men guilty of it will feel that they are attracting public attention; they will become more cautious how they overdrive and overwork their horses, particularly those that are old, sick, lame, and the terrible suffering inflicted by overloading *(that standing disgrace of this country)* will become less common; farmers will be ashamed to have their cattle come out in the spring mere skeletons; beating, starving, and freezing, and a

thousand other cruelties, will become more
rare; old, stray, and abandoned animals will be
taken better care of, or mercifully killed; birds
and their nests will be protected; and not only
will the laws in relation to the animals be en-
forced, but public sentiment will place in almost
every home advocates to plead their cause, and
to make known the cruelties which are inflicted
upon them.

The utopia for which Henry Bergh and George Angell
fought all their lives is not yet here. But they assured the
respectability of their cause. The leading citizens in many
communities list animal rescue and humane efforts of all
kinds among their regular charities or good works. Broad-
way, television, and Hollywood stars are always available to
work on committees, geography allowing, and I have sat on
boards and councils and taken part in conferences and hear-
ings with some of the most familiar names and faces in
America. Unabashedly, they are workers in the humane
movement. The legacy is almost certainly from two sources.
These people are animal lovers and are repaying a debt, the
debt of companion animal bonding. They are also more
comfortable in their very visible work as a result of the
groundwork laid down before, during, and after the Civil
War, by Henry Bergh and George Angell, the sensitive aristocrats and their philosophical heirs. Dogs have had few
friends their equal.

The dog has fitted into the human picture so tightly for
so long it would be too much to hope that no problems

would develop. The problems, however, have almost inevitably been with dog owners, not with dogs.

Rabies, a disease which despite two known human survivors is still generally considered 100 percent fatal by epidemiologists, can be transmitted from any mammal to any mammal, as far as we know, and that includes us. In many parts of the world, including the United States, it is always present just below the surface.

Since a dog is a mammal, it can contract rabies from a variety of wild animals, including, commonly, in the United States, wolves, coyotes, foxes, bats, raccoons, and skunks. Because dogs approach human beings more readily than any but the sickest wild animals do, dogs have traditionally carried rabies to human beings. But there has long been a vaccine for rabies. The agonies of the shots are much over-rated and are far less worrisome than a disease that is 100 percent fatal. (I have taken thirty-four rabies shots personally after a single bat bite and I know whereof I speak. Nice? No. Better than dying? Yes.)

Most people are stunned to learn that according to the Center for Disease Control (CDC) in Atlanta, Georgia, the number-one reportable public-health problem in the United States today is dogbite. There are over forty thousand dogbites reported in New York City alone every year, and it is because of rabies that these figures are known. It may have been decades since the last case of rabies was recorded, but dogbite reports are still required by health authorities. What is the cause of dogbite?

There are several factors, but crime is perhaps foremost among them. Dogs are many things, as I have tried to indicate throughout, and not the least of these things is a reaction to human society. If we feel belittled by our human condition we extend and enlarge our condition by possessing things, dogs among them, that make us bigger. Just as lizards inflate their throats to intimidate would-be predators, so we inflate ourselves to deter our attackers, whether the attack is aimed at our person, our goods, or our egos. We enlarge ourselves with dogs, and the fear of a mounting crime rate has Americans running around outdogging themselves to an incredible degree. Although most dog owners live in an urban or suburban setting, most dogs owned today are large and many are aggressive. Far too many of these are undertrained.

The breeding of dogs can take many forms. To some it is a science, to some an art, to many a hobby and a sport, but to a great many people it is a business. All across the United States and Canada there are pet shops that range from little fly-specked operations to elaborate emporiums in shopping malls. Almost all pet shops have this in common—they don't breed puppies themselves.

There are two basic sources of dogs for most pet shops: the incidental backyard local breeder, or Kansas City International Airport! Every Monday and Tuesday night—actually Tuesday and Wednesday morning, between two and five o'clock—hundreds and hundreds of puppies are assembled at KCI and carried east, west, north, and south by Trans World Airlines. There is supposed to be veterinary inspection by the Department of Agriculture, but when I went to KCI to see the phenomenon for myself, the TWA workers told me that it had been many months since a DA veterinarian had been seen. "They don't like those hours; the puppies are gone by five in the morning," commented one airline employee. It has gotten so bad that the TWA employees have taken it upon themselves to inspect the puppies and routinely turn away any that appear to be sick or in poor condition. These are the puppies heading for pet shops. But I must move back another step.

The puppies that appear at KCI are brought there by middlemen who drive around Kansas and Missouri picking up puppies from mass-producing breeders. Having experienced the disdain and rejection of TWA employees, they don't bother bringing unhealthy puppies to the airport. Some of them have purchased superannuated buses from the Greyhound Line (an irony!) and taken the seats out. One hundred and twenty puppies can be carried on a bus, and these are driven across the country and dropped off at pet shops along the way. A puppy may be on that bus in an orange crate for as long as ten days.

There is a federal law that says that puppies under eight weeks of age cannot be shipped interstate, but the middlemen who come between the mass producers and the pet shops regularly advertise that they ship at six weeks. Now I must move back another stage.

The mass producers (one advertised not long ago that he had sixty-four breeds for sale) are frequently retired pig or chicken farmers who have some shacks and can use extra income. Someone recently observed that there are more dogs in the chicken houses of Missouri than chickens. I visited some of these breeding colonies and found that bitches with their litters were often kept in wire-bottomed cages stacked three and four deep. Feces, urine, drinking water (filthy), and food (frequently inappropriate) drained down on the bitches and litters below. It was a series of pestholes, not kennels, that I saw and filmed for television.

Before putting all of this in a final context, let us look at the role of the American Kennel Club and "papers" in this mess. Since these puppies often arrive in the pet shops with

papers—that is, a pedigree and an AKC registration form—
what is the AKC up to?

First, pedigree. Pedigree forms are given out by the pet-
food companies at no charge. Anyone can get one and fill
it out any way they want. No trick there. AKC registration
is another matter.

The American Kennel Club is a registry, not a national
police force. If I am a breeder in Kansas and have a German
shepherd bitch and a German shepherd dog, I can breed
them and, if they are AKC-registered, get registrations for
the puppies as well. It is all done by mail. Let us say that I
do that for several litters and then my dog dies. No one
knows that unless I choose to announce it. I might then put
a German shepherd-Siberian husky cross with the same
bitch and send in the same registration information for that
litter that I did for the previous ones. Who can know that
at 51 Madison Avenue (AKC headquarters)? Like any piece
of paper, an AKC litter registration form is as good as the
person who fills it in is honest. So puppies appearing in a
pet shop may or may not be purebred; their papers prove
nothing. In all fairness, the pet-shop owner can no more
know what went on in Kansas than you or I can, or the
American Kennel Club computer.

One more step—the pet shop. The owner has invested in
highly perishable merchandise. Not only is there danger
that his puppies may become sick and die, they are certain
to grow up, if they live. Small puppies are not only cute and
easy to sell, they are often too small to show important
faults like mixed bloodlines. By the very nature of its business, a pet shop must move puppies out fast. Alive or dead,
they will soon become liabilities.

Running a halfway decent pet shop is hard work. Cages
must be cleaned constantly, water dishes and food dishes

seen to every few hours. Pay is not high for employees, because the margin is low and sales are uncertain except just before Christmas. That inevitably means that a large percentage of the employees are likely to be high school kids with little or no professional experience with dogs. Their mandate is to move the inventory fast. Puppies enter the shop on a treadmill and are never allowed off it. More puppies are on order, cage space is limited, and the present inventory is growing every day, and *eating*.

Now into the scene come the customers. They know little about dogs, but they have a vague idea that if a dog has *papers* everything has to be somehow O.K. They come through the door with their children and are met by a high school kid who offers to show them any puppy they want. There are "get-acquainted" areas where kids and puppies can mix to see if they like each other. All kids like all puppies and virtually all puppies like all kids. The "get-acquainted" concept is sheer razzle-dazzle and has nothing to do with living with a dog for up to fifteen years or more. Pet shops rely on impulse buying.

The innocent adult, watching his or her youngster loving and being loved by a puppy, then asks if that breed makes a good apartment pet. The salespeople, used-car salesmen that they are, assure you of anything you want to be assured of. They show you papers. Some pet shops even have the temerity to add a hundred or more dollars to the price of a puppy if papers go with it, although all papers are supposed to be free except for the minimal AKC registration fee for change of ownership.

There we have it. Puppies produced under pigsty conditions, not socialized by the breeders, traumatized by being taken from their mothers weeks before they should be, further traumatized by early shipment, sold by clerks who so

much of the time don't have any idea what they are talking
about, sold to people who don't know what they are getting
into. Very often the breeding has been poor or worse. A pig
farmer in Missouri is not testing dogs for temperament and
is as likely to breed a dragon to a dragon as not. A poorly
bred, undersocialized, badly traumatized puppy of quite
possibly an inappropriate breed is placed in the hands of an
inexperienced owner.

The result? Our staggering dogbite statistics. Most people seem to have the impression that most bites are delivered by "wild dogs" running mad through our neighbor-
hoods. That is patently not so. At least 85 percent of all
dogbites in the United States involve people being bitten by
their own pets. It is an ironic and wholly unnecessary reverse twist on the ancient and proven concept of joy.

How, then, does one buy a dog and avoid these seemingly
endless pitfalls?

Buy from known breeders who can show you at least one
of the puppy's parents. A good professional breeder may
have one or two breeds to show you, but never anything
remotely like sixty-four. Anyone breeding more than a few
breeds, at the most, is likely to be the very mass producer
you are most anxious to avoid. It takes a lifetime of hard
work and almost no profit (probably a loss) to perfect a
distinguished line of dogs of one breed. Good breeders are
so cautious of their puppies that they are usually reluctant
to let them go to people they do not know. As a very safe
rule, the prospective dog owner should beware when anyone *tries* to sell them a dog. The more you have to beg to
buy, the better your chances are of having a fine pet, when
you are dealing with purebred dogs, at least.

How do you find a breeder? Virtually all breeds recognized by the American Kennel Club are represented by a

breed club. The name and address of the secretary of the club representing the breed you think interests you are available from the AKC. The clubs usually have a magazine or bulletin for their breed, and a few back copies of it will tell you who the breeders are and the current issue will tell you who has puppies for sale. Another very good way of getting to know your dogs is to attend all-breed shows. Spend the day meeting and chatting with people who represent the breeds you like. Meet some dogs and some dog people and get your name on their waiting lists. In time you will find the breed, the breeder, and the puppy you want. Since you may be spending up to fifteen years in the company of that dog, it is worth time and care up front to assure yourself of the puppy that will really suit your style of life.

There are other ways of getting yourself a puppy, too. Purebred dogs are not inherently more intelligent than random-bred dogs. We have a staggering surplus of dogs and cats in this country. Somewhere between thirteen and fifteen million animals have to be destroyed every year simply because there are no homes for them. There is nothing at all wrong with adopting a stray, or a surplus puppy from a pound or humane shelter. You have to go by instinct, because you can't talk things over with a breeder, but I have personally known far too many fine dogs from shelters and pounds to question the logic of the process of adoption or the chances for an excellent result. There is an added value in adopting a surplus animal. Your children will have the enormous satisfaction of knowing that they are helping to save that animal's life. If you don't adopt it, it will in all likelihood be destroyed.

Many people of advanced years hesitate to take on a puppy because they are afraid it will outlive them or they will come to a point where they can't care for it. They dread what may happen to their pet if that happens to them. They deny themselves even though they may be very lonely. There is a solution to that: instant pet. Every animal shelter in this country has older animals that have been picked up as strays or turned in for any of a score of reasons, and they are usually all but unadoptable. Yet these animals are experienced pets, are almost always housebroken, may be obedience-trained, and don't require the exercise younger dogs do. They are excellent prospects for elderly people, and those are the people who should be encouraged by family and friends to take on a pet. It certainly helps eliminate at least some of the symptoms of the empty-nest syndrome.

If dog owners will select their dogs with care both by breed and by individual, will train them carefully in obedience, and will keep their dogs under control—and that means, of course, not wandering free—there is no reason why man and dog cannot continue to live together in harmony even in our most crowded cities for as long as both species survive. It is no great chore to clean up after your dog in the street; there is nothing wrong with keeping your dog on your own property in the suburbs and no reason to allow your dog to harry a farmer's livestock in the country. It really all comes down to good manners and good sense on the part of people. Dogs are seldom at fault when things go wrong.

9

Looking at Dogs: Personal Reminiscences

Probably the most famous statement ever made about a dog was made by Senator G. Vest of Missouri. He was representing a neighbor whose dog had been killed by another man. The man who suffered the loss was suing for $200, but when Vest got through with the jury the plaintiff was awarded $500 and the jury told the judge they wanted to send the dog killer to prison, something they couldn't do under the law. It took the jury two minutes to deliberate after hearing Vest's summation:

> Gentlemen of the Jury: The best friend a man has in this world may turn against him and become his enemy. His son and daughter that he has reared with loving care may become ungrateful. Those who are nearest and dearest to us, those whom we trust with our happiness and our

good name, may become traitors to their faith.
The money that a man has he may lose. It flies
away from him when he may need it most. Man's
reputation may be sacrificed in a moment of ill
considered action. The people who are prone to
fall on their knees and do us honor when success
is with us may be the first to throw the stone of
malice when failure settles its cloud upon our
head. The only absolutely unselfish friend a man
may have in this selfish world, the one that never
deserts him, the one that never proves ungrate-
ful or treacherous is his dog.

A man's dog stands by him in prosperity and
poverty, in health and sickness. He will sleep on
the cold ground, when the wintry winds blow and
the snow drives fiercely, if only he can be near his
master's side. He will kiss the hand that has no
food to offer, he will lick the wounds and sores
that come in encounter with the roughness of the
world. He guards the sleep of a pauper as if he
were a prince.

When all other friends desert, he remains.
When riches take wings and reputation falls to
pieces he is as constant in his love as the sun in
its journey through the heavens. If fortune drives
the master forth an outcast into the world,
friendless and homeless, the faithful dog asks no
higher privilege than that of accompanying him
to guard him against danger, to fight against his
enemies, and when the last scene of all comes,
and death takes his master in its embrace and his
body is laid away in the cold ground, no matter
if all other friends pursue their way, there by his

graveside will the noble dog be found, his head
between his paws and his eyes sad, but open in
alert watchfulness, faithful and true even to
death.

The wonder of it all is that Senator G. Vest didn't become
President of the United States! That statement to the jury
has been printed times beyond counting and is today on a
monument outside of the courthouse in Missouri where the
speech was made.

Of course, Senator Vest was engaging in some pretty
finely honed histrionics. He was pandering to the sentimentality of his jurors, and it worked. He was a skilled orator,
obviously, and he pulled out all the stops. The funny thing
is, so much of what he said was just plain true. Call it Victorian sentimentality, but recognize its truth. Dogs have been
very good friends for a long time. And they are often about
as faithful as Senator Vest suggested. That is why they are
still with us. They are very demanding of love themselves,
but they meet our demands for love, which are often
stronger and more desperate, even if subtler, than theirs
are.

One of the dog stories that always intrigued me has been
claimed by a good many places, Canada and Russia included, but the real source of the legend is Snowdonia in
North Wales. I went there to see for myself. The name of
the town is Beddgelert (pronounced beth-gel-aert), which
means "Gelert's grave." On the outskirts of this gray and
somber mountain village of fieldstone and slate is a grave
surrounded by a rusting iron fence. Inside the fence is the
marker that tells the story of Gelert, the faithful hound.
Traditionally, the site is said to be his grave.

Prince Llewelyn, Gelert's master, lived eight hundred to

a thousand years ago, and his home stood where Beddgelert is now located. He had a great hound whose breed we do not know, and that hound was destined to go down in history and folklore. One day Llewelyn was going hunting and called for Gelert, who for some reason did not appear. Eventually Llewelyn rode off alone. When he returned a few hours later, Gelert greeted him at the door. The great hound was covered with blood.

The prince dismounted and rushed into the building, directly to his son's bedroom. It was a shambles. The crib was on its side, and although the child was nowhere to be seen his blanket and crib linen were as bloody as the hound. In a fit of rage, the prince drove his sword through the dog. As the dog lay dying, Llewelyn heard a noise and leaped over the crib. His son was there, unharmed, and beside him was the body of a great wolf with its throat torn out. The story says that Prince Llewelyn never smiled again.

Not too many dogs have been immortalized as Gelert has with a whole town named after him, a handsome monument erected to his memory. There is no way of knowing, of course, if the story is true, but again there is enough truth in the story so that it doesn't really matter whether the actual events took place long ago in Snowdonia or not. Again sentimentality unbridled, but the awful truth is that dogs have been taking a bum rap from man almost as long, we surmise, as they have been our companions.

There have been bizarre twists to the bum-rap syndrome. In the early 1840s in England, it became fashionable and profitable, apparently, to steal dogs. An act was finally brought before Parliament to elevate the dog's value to that of livestock to make the punishment fit the crime. An opening statement said:

The greedy audacity with which professional dog-dealers and dog-stealers continue to
steal every species of the canine race, either for
the purpose of sale or extortion, involving alike
a serious loss of valuable property, and inflicting
the deepest anguish by the cruelties practiced on
the faithful companions of individuals of all
classes, from Her Majesty on downwards has
long been a source of public complaint and in-
dignation and has led to serious considerations
as to the expediency of extending to dogs the
same protection which the law affords to horses,
sheep, or other animals not more valuable in the
eyes of society.

There followed a petition to Parliament signed by three
dukes, one duchess, three marquesses and one marchio-
ness, twelve earls and one countess, two counts, and five
viscounts. There was as well a long list of sirs, honorables,
admirals, and generals and assorted lesser military officers
on down the list. It was a collection of big guns fighting to
protect dogs.

There then followed the list of recent complainants
who had lost dogs to dognappers. That, too, was an impressive list: His Royal Highness Prince George of Cambridge, H.R.H. the Duke of Cambridge, Count Kiel-
mansegge, Count Leodoffe, Viscount Loftus . . . page
after page of wealthy, royal, and variously titled people,
all of them victims of a peculiar crime that above all else
deprived them of the companionship of their dogs. After
each name was the amount of money they had paid in
ransom for the return of their pets. In all, the one list
showed 977 pounds, 4 shillings, and 6 pence extorted, an

enormous amount of money in the first half of the nineteenth century.

Petnapping still goes on, of course, and probably always
will, but somehow the epidemic of dog thefts from the
wealthy and the titled was brought under control in England, for the matter received relatively little attention toward the end of the century. Still, we can imagine the
stealthy sneak thief scaling walls of great estates not to steal
Turners and Gainsboroughs, not in pursuit of Georgian
silver or Limoges tureens, but in pursuit of dogs. One sus-
pects the victims of these night assaults would have preferred to see the silver and the china go rather than their
pets.

To try to reconstruct or comment on the history of man
and dog and remain clinical about that historical interaction
is a difficult task. Sentimentality has seeped through every
crack, permeates every layer of fabric; it runs as a theme
throughout it all. As I think back over my own life I can view
it as a chain of dogs and dog-related events, and each taught
me a lesson, often about myself. There has been much more
than dogs, of course—other animals, naturally, and people,
marriage, children, career, sickness, travel, adventure, perhaps—but always dogs. They were always there, links from
age to age, place to place, stage to stage. I am not sure I can
even recall all of them by name, there have been that many.

The first dog of which I have any memory at all was, as
I have already recounted, a Boston terrier and was on site
before I was born. I don't know how long he lasted, but I
do remember him. He was the first dog I touched, the first
that ever licked me, but before I could judge the experience
he was gone. Certainly, though, the total experience was
positive, for it was he who must have marked me with a very
gentle scar on my heart. A wire fox terrier (they were com-

monly called wirehaired fox terriers then) was around for a long time; that was Bozo. I believe I was about eight when he died. Not long ago I went back to look at that house where the fox terrier and I grew up together. It was strange. I felt he should still have been there. That fox terrier taught me the meaning of faith and loyalty.

The fox terrier was replaced by a collie puppy. That was to be a short, sad event. I remember kneeling beside that collie in the front yard as he lay dying. He was still a puppy, but he had somehow gotten a chicken bone and it had ripped him up inside. He was finally put down by a veterinarian, but he was almost dead by that time. I learned about mortality from that puppy. It was shocking to learn that the young could die, to come to know how fragile it all is, especially life.

When my older brother was thirteen—that would have made me about eight and a half—Peter arrived. He was an English cocker spaniel, all black with reddish-brown markings, perfectly balanced accents over the eyes, on the cheeks, and on the legs. He was a magnificent animal and was so close to human it was frightening. We moved from the country town of Methuen, Massachusetts, to Boston while we had Peter, and I remember the day he was hit by a car as he rushed off our apartment-house lawn to greet me coming home from school. He ran back onto the grass and promptly vomited. Our family pediatrician was coming that day, and he examined Peter's leg and splinted it. It probably wasn't even broken. As long as Peter lived—and that was to a ripe old age, approaching fifteen, as I recall—he would begin limping the moment he was scolded or thought he was about to be. Otherwise, his leg was fine. He never forgot the sympathy he had gotten while splinted, and although I can't determine with exactitude what intelligence is needed to develop a ruse like a fake limp, it seems to me it must be considerable. I suppose it is always possible that it wasn't intelligence but something rather more Pavlovian than that. Still, I like to think he was a very clever dog.

I do remember this dog very clearly, because my teenage years were particularly rough ones. I could trust Peter as I could trust no one else, nothing else, then in my life. He listened and listened and listened. He slept with me, sat with me, walked with me, looked up at me, and never once judged. Everyone else did judge me, and not too favorably at that. Peter was an anchor I really don't know what I would have done without.

World War II came when Peter was about five years old and I was thirteen. My older brother went off to the army, and Peter became all mine. He was my constant companion until I went in the army myself and was still there when I was discharged and headed off for college. He finally died when I was in school far from Boston. That one little dog with his fake limp as needed seemed to span a major portion of my life. From well before I was ten through all of high school, the army, and much of my college career, that dog remained unchanging, always pleasant, always grateful for so much as a touch. Few people have had better friends than that. By the time Peter's life had run its course I was locked into dogs forever. I am not sure I ever had a choice.

After college there was another army hitch (the Korean mess), then first jobs, then marriage. Only then was it possible to consider another dog. My wife and I chose a particularly handsome black miniature poodle. Because my wife, Jill, had been a ballet dancer and instructor, that poodle was named Tutu. Looking back, perhaps that dreadful name (yech!) was what turned him bad, for Tutu was the only dog in my life that I really failed with. He was a biter, a hopelessly cranky and assaultive animal. We tried everything we knew and nothing worked. He wasn't a fear biter, he was a mean biter. He had the heart of a dragon when all around him was the offering of love. If Jill got up to use the bathroom in the middle of the night, Tutu would move into her place, and there was no way she could get back into bed without waking me up to help her. I couldn't push Tutu off without being bitten. I would cock my legs and kick him so fast and hard from under the covers that he would fly out of bed and halfway across the room. Then Jill could rejoin me. It sounds silly now, but we really did not want to fail with that dog. We did. He went.

The experience with Tutu taught me a lesson. There are dogs, as much as we hate to admit it, that simply are not worth the price of admission, just as there are people in that category. (I first heard that expression applied to people by Helena Curtis, author of the best standard college biology text in use in America today. I think it one of the most apt expressions I have ever heard.) There are so many really fine dogs, both purebred and random-bred, that need homes that I personally think it is seldom worth the trouble to try to convert a really nasty dog into a nice one. It so seldom works. In Tutu's case, my paramount canine failure, we got him when he was eight weeks old. The little rotter was trying to bite by ten weeks and was succeeding by the time he was fifteen weeks. If he didn't like something, he bit the person nearest to him. Kindness, understanding, love (for a while), and near brutality all failed. Some people really are awful, and so are some dogs. I tried to understand that little devil, but nothing worked. Tutu was born with a screw loose or perhaps even missing.

After the failure with Tutu, I bought Jill a pug. Her beloved Boston terrier (all of us who grew up in Boston had

a beloved Boston terrier at some time or other), Pixie, had
been claimed by the great kennel master in the sky, and a
pug seemed a likely breed to try next. Winnie was a good
dog, although for some reason he never quite got under my
skin the way Peter the English cocker had. I think some
dogs, in this case Peter, like some people come to mean so
much they almost spoil us for the other emotional opportunities in life. At any rate, Winnie lived on to a good age
and was pleasant enough. While Winnie was still in residence, Bridgette joined us. Now, there was an absolutely
remarkable animal.

Biddy belonged to friends who were about to move to
Australia, and they needed a home quickly for their toy
poodle. She was not a happy dog, because the man of the
household was having a manhood crisis of some kind, and
to him a toy poodle was too little a dog, or something. (The
man weighed well over three hundred pounds.)

Whenever we visited that household, long before we ever
thought of Bridgette or Biddy becoming ours, there would
be a black flash and a blur as a toy poodle shot from under
the couch to under a chair to behind the drapes. She was
a thoroughly neurotic animal, beloved by her mistress and
despised by her master, in a house with no other animals
and very few human guests.

In time, of course, we accepted Bridgette, but with little
hope for her making it. We had Winnie the pug, and we had
several cats—and we had been told that Biddy hated cats.
The day came; Jill picked her up, and she stepped out of a
carrying case in the middle of our living room and looked
around. Our two kids came to inspect her, Winnie did, and
so did a couple of siamese cats. Biddy trembled, but she
held firm. There was a kind of fire inside. Not a blaze so
much as a warm glow.

Within a few days that little poodle managed a total transformation. The first evening she came to me and asked to sit in my lap. I complied. She began following the kids to see what they were up to, although in her own home she would never have gotten near them. One evening Jill and I were sitting watching television with Biddy on the couch between us.

"I thought this monster was supposed to hate cats," I recalled to Jill.

"She certainly doesn't hate ours," Jill observed. Then Jill called out, "Bridgette, there's a kitty over there, a kitty, kitty, kitty."

Biddy began barking furiously, leaped off the couch, and ran to the window in a rage. On the way she passed three cats. In fact, although she had learned that the word "kitty" was terrible, she did not have the foggiest notion what one was. So much for the hates in her life. All fake.

I don't think I have ever known a dearer dog than that little poodle. She lived for a long time, almost fifteen years, but then it was downhill every day with fewer functions under control, more fear and pain, and finally there had to be an awful decision. Biddy went to her reward. I shall always miss her and always have a very soft place inside for toy poodles. We have friends with several of them and variously refer to them *en fleet* as army ants or patio lice. As a Hollywood press agent in my wild youth I got to know a good many toy poodles in a great many extremely luxurious settings. I think Joan Crawford's last years were made more tolerable by her little poodle. She cherished it and it her, and many an evening I chatted with Joan with that poodle her only other companion. Amanda Blake, the beautiful Miss Kitty of television's *Gunsmoke* for almost twenty years, always keeps a veritable battalion (or posse) of toy poodles around. Barbara Walters adores hers, one I had the fun of getting for her. There are a great many others that fill my memories of people and places. Anyone who puts the size variety of that breed down simply does not know what he or she is talking about. A toy poodle is enough dog for any man, woman, or child, and a lot brighter than most. There simply can be nothing wrong with love, and that is a lesson any poodle, especially a toy, can teach anyone.

While Winnie and Biddy were both in residence, I first met Nel. She was, I would guess, about six months old and was probably a cross between a German shepherd and an airedale, although there were things about her that suggested some collie. There was terrier blood, though; the coat was, in fact, pure wiry earth dog.

I was sitting in our car outside our apartment house while Jill went in to send the baby sitter out for her ride home. I saw a puppy approaching people one after the other. There was something desperate about her movements, even in the dark, even at a distance. People pushed her aside; one man used his furled umbrella to shove her away. I rolled the window down and called to her. She bounded over and put her feet up on the window ledge. She was indeed desperate. She was so seriously dehydrated that when I took a handful of her scruff it remained standing. Her skin had lost its pliability. She was near death from starvation and thirst. I went inside, leaving the baby sitter to watch the car, and brought water and some steak out to the desperate puppy. She wolfed it all down. Heaven alone knows how long it had been since she had eaten. I didn't think it wise to take her in to the other dogs without knowing if she was carrying anything, and so I rang my in-laws, who lived nearby. They agreed to give the pup a home for the night, just for the night.

We never could find Nel's owners, although the fact that she was nervous about cars as long as she lived suggests that she may have been dumped from a car before I found her. She shook every time she was asked to climb aboard. Nel was spayed and sent to obedience school, and she remained the closest of canine friends for almost sixteen years. She was extremely protective of our children, and after we had built our house she would take up her position in the corridor that led to their bedrooms once they had gone off to bed. That was it. Guests had to use a bathroom at the other end of the house. No outsiders could go near the bedroom doors of those two small people she apparently felt she had been put on earth to protect. Nel Gwynn, as she came to be called, was all dog, pure dog, and if anyone ever has anything disparaging to say about random-bred dogs I need only think of her. While she was still alive we had her portrait painted. One ear went up and one went down, but her eyes went straight ahead. She had a fix on life and duty that any human being could learn from. Once she joined us she lived only the good life. I often wondered if she could remember anything that went before except by reflex, like the car.

Oomiac has just recently left us by reason of old age and intractable arthritis. She was a hopeless prostitute. She was a particularly lovely siberian husky that Jill and I found in a shelter in Virginia fourteen years ago or thereabouts. Her entire litter had been turned in by a breeder for reasons that are still not really clear. The shelter had done its best to find homes for them, but sled dogs have limited appeal in Virginia. Oomiac was the last one left. Each of the others had been put to sleep one at a time. Her sister had been the last to go just the day before. Oomiac was then about a year old and incredibly lovely to look at and as sweet as she could be. She was facing the firing squad the next day, and we just couldn't take it. We said we would take her, although we really did not need another dog. We never really do, if we are to be honest about it. The kennel boy, a kid of about seventeen, wept as he handed her over to us. We promised to give her a good home. He had wanted to have her, but his parents wouldn't let him.

Oomiac was never really our dog. She was anybody's dog, or everyman's dog. She discovered that the sound of hammers had special meaning. It meant another house was being built somewhere not too far off, and that meant workmen who brought lunches with them. Day after day our front yard would be littered with brown paper bags and wax paper as workmen, I am sure, scurried around looking for their peanut-butter-and-jelly sandwiches, perhaps never even suspecting that that nice, pretty husky that visited them so regularly was in fact a terrible thief.

Oomiac wanted to come inside only when there were electrical storms. She always wanted to be an outside dog, and judging from her size she had more than one home in the neighborhood. I can't imagine how many of us fed her every day, but she was happy and immensely pleasant, although her advanced years made her quite lame.

By this point in the Caras canine history we were living in the country, and that, along with our generally relaxed attitude toward kids and animals, created a tidal wave. There were Winnie, Biddy, Nel, and Oomiac, respectively a pug, toy poodle, random-bred, and siberian husky. That was when our daughter, Pamela, decided her first week's paycheck from her new job as a riding teacher could best be spent on . . . you guessed it, a dog. That was how we got Jeremy Boob, the golden retriever. I must confess, Pamela handled it like a pro. I was at this very typewriter when my study door flew open. Pamela entered carrying a huge golden puppy *and followed by several of her friends.* The plan, apparently, was that they would all stare me down if I got tough. It is very difficult to be hardheaded with half the youth in town staring at you. Anyway, Jeremy landed and is still alive and well, and I must admit he has proved just how gloriously gentle and responsive a golden retriever can be. They are not always breeding goldens as well today as they used to, so popular have they become. Jeremy came from a good old line—massive head, broad chest, lovely, absolutely saintlike disposition. His father, Junior Grossman, was just like him and appears to have sired half the goldens east of Hawaii. Junior Grossman led a good, full, rich life, and Jeremy was one of his paramount accomplishments.

Jeremy has been involved in a few social interactions with people and other dogs that are particularly interesting. He had the very bad habit of escaping from the fenced yard where most of our dogs are kept. When free, Jeremy heads for a special bus stop he knows where the school bus unloads a parcel of kids every afternoon at just about the same time. Jeremy, enjoying his temporary freedom, visits with the kids and picks his kid-for-the-day and follows him or her home. He usually scrounges a cookie or two, so the rumors that have drifted back to us suggest, and after a bit asks to be let out and heads home. Although there is very little traffic in our area, we do discourage roaming.

Jeremy wears a tag on his collar, of course, with our name and phone number and his name as well. It is a simple enough precaution. Apparently, on one of Jeremy's expeditions into other homes, other kitchens, the thoughtful mother of the child he had selected for the day felt the dog should not be turned loose. Checking the tag of the exceedingly agreeable Jeremy, she found it had rusted somewhat

and only Jeremy's last name, Boob, survived on that particular line. (It is a wonder Jeremy isn't rusted all over, considering the amount of time he spends diving in off our beach.
He is a retriever and knows retrievers belong in the water
no matter what the weather. Retrievers apparently feel they
should be either getting wet or drying out, twenty-four
hours a day.)

The phone call about Jeremy came and was taken by my
exceptionally English mother-in-law, who now lives with us
and helps manage what has become a kennel.

The voice on the other end was very clear: "I have your
Boob."

"I beg your pardon!" my mother-in-law answered. You
have never heard what those four words can sound like until
they have been delivered by Phyllis Langdon Smith Barclay,
who graduated from Mrs. Whatchamacallit's School for the
Daughters of Gentlemen in Henley-on-Thames. "You have
my what?"

"I have your Boob."

My son was dispatched immediately by his Nana to collect
his sister's dog, while I fixed my mother-in-law a glass of
sherry. "Whatever do you suppose possessed that woman!
My boob indeed."

Jeremy seemed ashamed when he was brought somewhat
reluctantly through the front door. I think my son must
have told him that he had stirred things up a bit.

Jeremy has always been able to find a common ground
with other animals and make a relationship, however unlikely it might appear, work. He loves cats, and although he
always found it humiliating he would let kittens attempt to
nurse on him. He was very patient, but if a golden retriever
can get red in the face he did.

We have never believed in keeping wild or exotic animals,

simply because we think it is a poor practice generally and a particularly bad example for us to set, however much we may have wanted one and felt we should be the exception to the rule. Our frustrated desires were temporarily satisfied from time to time when zoos asked us to take on an orphan. It was always heartbreaking to let them go when half grown, but at least the kids got the experience of handling lion cubs, a leopard for a short time, and a couple of mountain lions, not to mention owls and other waifs the zoos didn't have time for.

Jeremy always interacted well with these strange-smelling creatures with their strange and at times obnoxious habits. Lucy the mountain lion stayed for a number of months, and Jeremy had her number down cold. Each day we would let a herd of thundering dogs and one lone mountain lion out to run down to the beach. We followed not too far behind, and the animals all responded to an invitation to chase sticks. At least the dogs did. Lucy chased the dogs, but because she had been barked at for leaping onto tails she pretty well behaved herself. It was during the trip down to the beach where the dumb-show occurred every day, and *it always involved Jeremy.*

Our back door is 290 feet from the water. About halfway down, Lucy would inevitably remember what she was. Midway through the tangle of phragmites and beach plum, she would have a hot flash. *Hey, cat, you are not like the others. You are a mountain lion, a ferocious wild animal, a killer.* You could watch it like clockwork; it always happened in just the same way. The animals would all be bouncing and pirouetting down toward the beach when Lucy would haul up short. A bulb would light up over her head announcing the realization had come again. She would stop, her tail would puff, her hackles would rise, her ears would go back along her head, her lip would quiver, and out would come one of those escaping-steam sounds that old-timers said sounded like a grizzly bear being raped. It is a terrific wild sound. Really impressive.

That was where Jeremy would come in. You could watch the entire pantomime from a distance. He would stop dead in his tracks and turn to look at the fierce mountain lion all puffed, arched, and snarling. He would walk back to where she was displaying and sit down quite close to her and look. In a moment or two she would begin to feel foolish. I swear, if you could have heard the dialogue it would have gone like this.

"What are you supposed to be doing?"

"Snarl, spit, explode, snarl."

"Look, we're going down to the beach and play. You can come if you want or you can stay here like an idiot and do your mountain-lion bit. It's all the same to us."

(Halfheartedly) "Snarl? Spit?"

"You heard me. Have it your way. We'll be down on the beach when you get this out of your system. Nobody, by the way, is impressed."

Lucy would just about shrug. Her ears would come down, her tail hairs would deflate, the arch in her body would soften and then vanish, and within thirty seconds she would be running along beside Jeremy catching up with the other dogs.

Jeremy had his way with anything that ever came into our home. As long as it didn't jump on his tail when he was sleeping, it could hang in and play with the rest of them. That is what a golden retriever is supposed to be like—a gentleman, a diplomat, a friend to all who deserve his love.

I think Libby arrived or happened next. My daughter was

walking down the main street of our town one hot Fourth of July when she encountered a tearful little boy pushing a wheelbarrow fairly brimful with puppies.

"What's wrong?" Pamela asked, knowing full well she shouldn't.

"Snivel, snivel," came the reply. "My father says that if I don't find homes for these puppies by one o'clock he will drown them. Snivel, snivel."

The little hustler will probably sell that bridge in Brooklyn to an Eskimo trying to get a refund on the refrigerator he sold him the week before.

We got Liberty, in honor of our nation's birthday, and that has become shortened to Libbie. Libbie is everything thrown in together, including ex-dreadful. Always good-natured, she was the most destructive puppy I have ever known. But spaying and obedience class have done it again. Libbie is now a perfect pet.

In the middle of all this, Jill and I made a trip to London, and while there, for whatever reason I can't imagine, we bought a dog. We had both always wanted a real honest-to-goodness bulldog, and clearly England is the place to get one. English breeders are terribly conscientious, and we had fared very well indeed with a siamese cat we had bought the kids when we all lived there in the mid-'60s. We had gone over so I could work on the film *2001: A Space Odyssey*. All the pets had to stay home because of England's six-month quarantine law. We got the kids the cat from a very famous breeder and got to know a bit about British attitudes toward their pets. Getting the bulldog in London (although it had been bred and whelped in Wales, Pembrokeshire to be exact) seemed like a good idea at the time. In fact, it was. Glynnis Gay Girl was her pedigree name, but she became

Pudge to us. We considered appropriate Welsh names like Blodwyn, but somehow it was just good old descriptive Pudge when the smoke cleared.

We had learned that TWA allowed one small dog per cabin, pilot's ultimate option, if reservations were made in advance. We began checking flights and found the first flight on which the "dog seat" was open originated in Paris, not London, and left several days after we had planned. We changed our plans to suit the schedule, and Pudge flew home to America in style, sitting between Jill and me and yowling at the flight attendant every time she walked down the aisle. Pudge had learned that it was from her all good things flowed while aloft. She ate her way across the Atlantic by just being enchantingly noisy. The pilot was an animal lover and came back to visit with his noisy passenger as often as it was safe for him to do so. I am sure his friends on the flight deck thought he was suffering from a peculiar malady, so often did he desert them.

Pudge was a lovely creature, but proved a mixed blessing. She was fine with other animals, unless food was involved. Cats and other dogs could curl up and sleep with her—she was, after all, a giant hot-water bottle. But she would brook no nonsense when anything edible was in sight. Unfortunately, her jaws were like steel traps, for that is a peculiarity of the breed. Someone dropped some food on the floor and she and a kitten arrived at the same time. We are certain Pudge, who is not a fighter normally, did not mean to do it, but the kitten died of a fractured skull almost instantly. On another occasion another kitten suffered a similar injury but lived. Quite in error, we felt certain that we could keep Pudge if only we were careful about food. We were wrong.

Our son Clay had gotten himself a job in a veterinary hospital. It seemed we simply had to grow our own veterinarian if we were to survive financially. At that hospital he found Andrew, a tiny, very assertive, nondescript little puppy, but Clay loved him dearly. Andrew and Pudge arrived at a fallen scrap of food at the same time, and Andrew's jaws were so badly crushed that he had to be put down. Then we knew that Pudge, although we adored her and she would never, never bother a human being, simply had to have a home with fewer small animals who could be accidentally annihilated by the touch of her power-driven jaws.

Pat Derby and Ed Stewart were visiting in New York at the time, and though turning Pudge over to lion trainers did seem an excessive reaction, they loved Pudge and the deal was made. It wasn't really a deal, since no money was involved. Simply, they would offer Pudge a great home on their wild-animal ranch in California. Ed promised to play the "bee game" with her once a day. That involved raising your finger high in the air and saying, "Pudge, here comes a bee." You brought your finger down slowly, buzzing like a bee and not caring a wit if everyone around you thought you totally mad. While waiting for the "bee" to sting her, Pudge went fairly mad with anticipation, spinning in circles, barking, pretending stark terror. You simply touched her with your finger after perhaps thirty seconds of insane buzzing and shouted, "Gotcha." Pudge loved it, and Ed quickly learned how to do it quite well. He made a good bee, in fact.

Pat and Ed raise everything from elephants and Siberian tigers to grizzly bears and mountain lions for use on television and in the movies. They are the most humane trainers I have ever known, and it seemed fairly certain that an elephant, a seven-hundred-pound tiger, a thousand-pound grizzly bear, and assorted other large animals would man-

age to hold their own against even Pudge's accidental transgressions.

Pudge did live a nice long life in California, at least long
for a bulldog—close to ten years. They tell stories about
her, my favorite being close to a tragedy, but one that does
reveal the true bulldog character. One day, Pudge, for reasons known only to her, wandered down Pat and Ed's driveway. Since it was about a mile long I don't know what
possessed the great bowlegged one, but she did it and got
herself hit by a pickup truck. She limped back up that long
mile and flopped down in Pat and Ed's living room. She was
known to the rancher who had unavoidably, as it turns out,
hit her, and he rode over on horseback later that evening
to see if Pudge was all right. Pudge bit his horse.

Bulldogs are a very special breed. Until she died, Pudge
played the bee game, loved everybody she ever met, and
never challenged another animal unless food fell between
them. I think, under those conditions, Pudge would have
taken on the elephant, the tiger, the grizzly bear, and all the
rest.

After Pudge killed Clay's poor little Andrew, Clay decided he would like not only to get another puppy of his
own but to show one. His sister, Pamela, who had graced
our lives with Jeremy Boob and Libbie, was showing horses.
Clay would show dogs. It seemed like a perfectly reasonable
idea at the time and we asked him what breed he had in
mind. He said he wasn't sure, not telling us that he was, in
fact, almost sure.

I suggested that since the Westminster Kennel Club
Show was coming up at Madison Square Garden he take two
days off from school and spend those two days and evenings
at the Garden looking over all the breeds. I also suggested
that he look at the small terriers, especially the little Nor-

wich, which I consider a very good kid's dog. At the time, Clay was just fifteen and was spending part of each week, the bulk of it, really, at school in New York City and only weekends and holidays at the country house. That meant his puppy would have to travel back and forth, and a moose with a flea collar could be a nuisance in a car.

Off to Madison Square Garden he went. For some years I have been announcing that great dog show, but I had not yet started doing that. I was, however, taping a one-hour sports spectacular for CBS (that was during my pre-ABC days) with Pat Summerall. Clay and I bumped into each other with regularity both days and evenings. He would not confess to a preference. The day after the show, Wednesday, both before he left for school and after he came home, Clay was close-mouthed. Then on Thursday, after school, he asked if he could talk about dogs with me.

"And what nice little terrier-type appeals to you?" I asked hopefully.

"How do you feel about bloodhounds, Dad?"

"Bloodhounds! That is literally a moose!"

An argument ensued that must have raged back and forth for fifteen or twenty seconds, and then Jill, Clay, and I were pouring over books compiling a list of the best bloodhound strains in the country.

In fact, I had always loved the breed and we have since owned fifteen of them, but at that time I had had little exposure to good examples. I recalled that some months before Westminster, Clay had attended a sportsman show and spent time at a state police exhibit that featured a trailing bloodhound. He had come home singing the dog's praises.

I called Jack LaFore, then president of the American Kennel Club, and Bob Taylor, then chairman of the Westmin-

ster Kennel Club Show, and asked them who had the best
bloodhounds in the country. They both recommended the
Rectory Kennels in Owens Mills, Maryland, run by the Rev.
George Sinkinson, an Episcopalian priest, and his wife,
Jackie. I put a call through to them, and yes they had a
puppy but no they wouldn't agree to sell it to us until we
had passed their critical examination. (The story of what the
Sinkinsons put us through, how I nearly blew the whole deal
by hitting the soup before grace after they had invited us to
dinner, is recounted in a book called *Yankee.*)

To make a long story somewhat shorter, we did get Yankee Patriot ("Yankee"), and Jill went quite mad, although
she had always professed to be a cat person. Any less catlike
dog than the bloodhound I can't imagine, but she was
quickly hooked and began showing Yankee for Clay, then
his daughter, Penny, then Trinity, then Mandy, and now we
have puppies. I think the present bloodhound count is ten.

The Jack Russell terriers came in time, and a couple of
short-term visitors like Nickie the cocker spaniel, but not
too many dogs can handle the Caras scene of lots of cats,
lots of dogs, and lots and lots of people. When a waif has
not been able to make it here we have always managed to
find it a good home. Tigger the papillon, previously discussed, also came for a stay.

It certainly could be argued by any reasonable person
that we have had an excessive number of animals, and I
strongly suspect it has cost us the friendship of people who
don't enjoy our kind of home scene and thus avoid us. I do
know that I can draw lines through good times and bad,
especially bad, and remember some if not all of the dogs
who have been friends, good friends. My wife, our two
children, and I have been tied together by any number of

things—annual photographic safaris in Africa, an art collection, interest in antiques—but our sharing of the responsibility and joy of companion animals has been of enormous
importance. My son is not going to be a veterinarian after
all, but is now in medical school. Still, both of our kids come
home every chance they get, they ask after their old pets and
our new ones every time they call, which is several times a
week, and they have looked upon our four-legged family
members as just that, in some strange way siblings.

When I write I am locked away in a soundproof study and
Yankee the bloodhound, now going on eight, is always with
me. Every now and then he decides that it is time to interact.
He comes over and puts his chin on my knee. I stop what
I am doing and without any feeling of self-consciousness,
we talk. The dog listens, of course, and I talk, but we interact. This great dog is my close friend. Peter listened to me
when I was a very badly shaken teenager wondering if I
could survive and meet the expectations of everyone
around me; Yankee listens to me now. I have never been
judged by a dog, and there have been lots of times in my
life when I needed not to be.

People tell me about their dogs and other companions.
They write to me, send me pictures, share their pride and
their grief. If you write about animals and talk about animals
long enough, that is bound to be the case, because animal-
oriented people are sharers by nature. One day the chief of
police of our village, one of his officers, and the officer's son
dropped in to see the bloodhound puppies. The chief had
a story to tell.

Not terribly long ago, he was driving in his police car when an alarm came over the radio—*rape in progress.* Racing to the address given as fast as he could drive on country roads, he leaped out of his car to be greeted by the frantic screams of a woman coming from the house. He drew his gun and approached in the shadows. He could see the screen door was torn open. Making a quick dash for it, he went right through the door himself, assuming the classic combat pistol stance as he landed in the room. A middle-aged woman was backed up against the wall clutching her toy poodle bitch while a very excited male Labrador retriever tried to get at the little dog, which was obviously in an enticing condition. Chief Stonemetz was laughing so hard he could hardly coordinate his own efforts to pull the retriever away.

Sometimes the mail is a little difficult to answer. Not terribly long ago I received a letter from a woman, and I quote it here:

> *Dear Mr. Caras,*
> *My neighbor is having an unnatural relationship with her dog. She kisses it on the mouth. She used to have a German shepherd, but now she has a doberman pinscher. Do you think this is right?*

And another:

> *Dear Mr. Caras,*
> *Please, please, please help me. My veterinarian is a crook. I didn't used to think so, but now I do. He is trying to collect $8.00 from me for giving my German shepherd mix a distemper shot. He has been taking care of the dog for years and knows it has a perfectly good disposition.*

And yet another:

> *Dear Mr. Caras,*
> *I read your article in* **Ladies' Home Journal** *and I think we should spay and neuter our dogs, too. My husband says I can spay our little poodle bitch but he gets very angry when I want to have our male retriever mongrel castrated. He gets so angry. What is wrong with him? Can you talk to him for me? My phone number is . . . Please call right away because my husband really is furious with me. Don't call collect.*

I get regular requests to act as referee in divorce actions, to decide who gets the dog or cat. One letter was quite angry:

> *Dear Mr. Caras,*
> *I hate my husband. He is a rotten bastard. He isn't even decent enough to have a girl friend. He has a boy friend. He has lied and lied and lied and he wants a divorce, but he also wants our two cats. No way. We're staying married. I have always loved those cats more than him. What do you think?*

One woman wrote to me to tell me her dog Favor had died and she wanted to give the same amount of money she had spent maintaining Favor each year to a humane shelter in his memory. She wanted me to recommend a shelter. Since the return address was only a couple of miles from where I live, I decided to spare myself one letter and phone her. The somewhat startling conversation went like this:

> *"Mrs. Jones?"*
> (Rather brusque) *"Yes."*
> *"This is Roger Caras. I am calling about your letter."*

"What letter?"
"About Favor. I'm sorry about your loss."
"How did you know about Favor?"
"You wrote to me."
"No, I didn't."
*"Well, in fact you did. You wanted me to recommend
a shelter where the money could go in his memory."*
"How did you know about that?"
"Well, as I said, you wrote to me."
"Who is this?"
"Roger Caras."
"Never heard of you." Click.

On another occasion I was recording my radio show when
a desk assistant slipped me a note saying there was a Mr.
Terhune phoning from New Jersey. I jotted down instructions for the young man to get Mr. Terhune's number and
I would call him back in a few minutes. My recording time
was almost up.

After coming out of the studio, I went directly to the
phone. It was rather exciting, I thought. Albert Payson Terhune, who wrote *Lad: A Dog,* must be dead, but perhaps this
was his son or grandson. I was pleased with the call.

A very gruff voice came on the line.
"Yeh."
"May I speak to Mr. Terhune, please."
"Who is this?"
"This is Roger Caras at CBS"—where I was at the time—
*"and I am returning Mr. Terhune's call of about fifteen
minutes ago."*
"Who?"
"Roger Caras at CBS."
"Yeh, well, this is Mr. Terhune and I never heard of you."

"Well, I did get a call just a few minutes ago—"
Click.

One has to learn to accept blows to the ego. Some dog people are terrific and some apparently live rather intense internal lives and offer rather less to those of us on the outside than we feel we might need. Over the years I have heard from any number of people who approve of me because their pets do. I am never certain what that means, but I am always glad to hear that people are communicating with their pets. And at my age I'll take any approval I can get.

Many letters are funny, often very funny indeed, and others are sad. A few are threatening because I love animals too much or too little. If you are the recipient of three hundred letters a week you can be certain of one thing. You can't win. One letter in particular seemed to please my wife and kids. It began: "You are an impotent, child-molesting, homosexual communist out for a quick buck." After that it got nasty. My kids wanted to frame it and hang it in the kitchen. I fought and got it back.

A surprising number of letters rage against dogs because they have the temerity to eat protein, they need about fifty times as much per pound of bodyweight as we do. The letters, perhaps 1 or 2 percent of the total, argue that our pets are taking that protein away from starving children and contributing to worldwide famine. They also state that our own food bills are higher because the shopper in the market must compete with wealthy dog owners. There is absolutely no merit to either argument. Consider these facts:

Dry kibble foods get most of their protein from corn and soy beans. Very little comes from the slaughterhouse, and what does is waste, bone meal, dried blood, and other substances that human beings will not eat or cannot eat by law.

Federal law defines "meat" as muscle tissue only. Steak is meat, heart is meat, but liver is not and kidneys are not; all of the organ tissues fall under the classification of meat by-products. Some meat by-products, like tripe, sweetbreads, liver, and kidneys, we eat, but a great deal of the rest is not deemed fit for human consumption. If anyone seriously suggests that nose pads, penis sheaths, vulvas, anuses, ears, and hooves are being denied starving children by our dogs I don't think I for one would care to engage in a protracted argument.

The second complaint: we have to pay more for meat because of what our dogs eat. Again, nonsense. We pay *less.* The explanation for that is simple. At one time, slaughterhouse operators or "dressers" got about two cents a pound for scrap that went into chickenfeed and fertilizer. Now, dog-food manufacturers pay as much as seventeen or eighteen cents a pound for the same material. That means the dresser is getting more per carcass processed and does not have to take his higher costs per animal on the hoof out as much on us as he would if the dog-food companies hadn't multiplied his take per pound of inedible meat by-products by eight to nine times. No children anywhere are being starved or imperiled or deprived by your dog and mine.

One last thought: what about all that corn and soya? That could go into human food. It could, except it wouldn't be grown. We can grow as much corn and soya as we can sell and at that point cut off production. There is no shortage of either product. The corn and soya used by the pet-food industry is grown for it, and that means extra cash in the farmer's pocket. The statement holds—human beings are not in competition with dogs for nutrition.

I have corresponded with literally thousands of people

about their dogs. Every day of my life I am stopped on the street, in elevators, in stores, and told about or asked about dogs. Requests for information or pleas to share come by phone and are sometimes as funny as the mail, sometimes as sad. In my business you learn to listen and hope to care. The one thing you must never do, for the sake of the people whom you meet and who think they need your help and for your own sake as well, is stop caring. When you stop caring you lose something precious, because it is not only animals you have stopped caring about but people. Dogs need help far less often than dog owners. By and large, I find dogs are better copers than people and philosophically a lot more stable.

In retrospect—and you are allowed to delve in retrospect when you have seen that shady side of fifty, as I did several years ago—I don't know what happened, how it came to me, or what, if anything, I could have done about it. In a great many people, exaggerations of normal twists, talents, and turbulence appear. We can all drum our fingers or hum "America the Beautiful," but then there is Arthur Rubinstein. He is an exaggeration. Most of us can play rudimentary chess at some stage of our growing up, but then there is Bobby Fischer. Most of us get angry, often very angry, then there is Charles Manson. All of us can put a pen or pencil to paper and draw an apple, however unappealing, but then there was Van Gogh. Whatever we do—walk, jump, climb, write, cook, spell, swim, joke, pound nails, or love dogs—there is someone somewhere, and more likely lots of people, who do it far, far better than we do; they are exaggerations of normal human pursuits. Some are idiot savants, although I suspect few people like to think of themselves that way, and some are just blessed with a gift. I don't know what gland, muscle, hormone, or sympathetic system

governs the ability to relate to animals, but mine was en-
larged, I should think, from birth. I was lucky enough to
marry a girl with the same problem. Perhaps not all that
surprisingly, we raised two children who are more or less in
the same fix. I am not certain whether it was heredity, a
swelling, or strictly environmental influence. Whatever the
facts, however it came about, we ended up surrounded by
hundreds of people and scores of animals. It has been fun.

I am as confounded by dogs as I am indebted to them. I
won't try to outdo Senator Vest, whom I quoted earlier, but
dogs have played a remarkable role in human development
and in my own life. The Carnivora to which they belong
contain some of the most and some of the least attractive
animals that bear backbones—weasels of all kinds, including skunks; viverrid, including the genet, civet, and mongoose; the cats, of course, from small, tabby-sized jungle
cats to one of the greatest of all the living carnivores on
land, the Siberian tiger; the hyenas; the bears; the Procyoni-
dae, which include the raccoon, and, of course, the canines.

In one or two species or subspecies of canine, the wolves,
there lay an astounding set of genes. They were made of
rubber, and like all good rubber they have a memory of
their own. If you stretch a rubber band it remembers and
goes back into its own private shape. Dog genes are like
that. If you take the pressure off, the selective breeding, like
the elastic band, the genes all start slipping back toward
their original shape. We don't make permanent changes in
canine genes, we simply borrow them and deflect them and
keep them deflected as long as we want. That gives us our
bloodhounds and our borzoi, our bulldog and our basenji.
The cocker spaniel and corgi, the collie and the keeshond,
are individual concepts of perfection available for as long as
we want to maintain them, and then, quietly, they will slip

backward toward the wolf via some other earlier form. Every one of our glorious breeds is only a few years away from the millennia-old cave dog early taken from the loins of a wolf. All of that is as it was somehow meant to be. The joy of it all, the wonder of it, is that man found the wolf and did his early experiments, something that still leaves me with mouth agape. How did that extraordinarily unsophisticated Early Stone Age man, or even Middle Stone Age man, know how to breed selectively? That is precisely what he did.

Consider this. If man found just the right kind of wolf or two before he even made really good flint skinners and millennia before he invented the bow and arrow, if he learned how to breed selectively and arrive at animals as diverse but as pure as the greyhound, the saluki, and the samoyed before he knew there were sperm, much less chromosomes, much less genes, could it have been foreordained? What would man have done without the dog? One thing—he would have faced a different rate of growth for his own cultures and economies, and perhaps a completely different image of himself. Man and dog, an inevitable mix, is a powerful reason for celebration.